THE DEER SHOT BACK

And Other Hunting Tales

Illustrated by
CEDAR SANDERSON

Published by Sanderley Studios.

www.cedarwrites.com

Cover Art and Design, and Interior Illustrations by Cedar Sanderson

Edited by Cedar Sanderson

❀ Created with Vellum

CONTENTS

DEDICATION AND FOREWORD

It's been years since I was able to go hunting, or even fishing, and I haven't set a trap since I was a teenager. Far too long. One thing about this project is that I've been reminded why I hunted. It wasn't just for the meat, although as Brennan Hankins mentions in his FortyMile Caribou Blues, my family were subsistence hunters. We filled the freezer, and there were a few lean years where without that food, survival got dicey.

For my family, this was the case for generations. I learned my first lessons about hunting and respect for the creatures we pursued from my Great-Grandfather, Warren Vanderburg. By the time I came along, he was in the twilight of his years, and often ill with the leukemia that would claim his life much later. However, I have early and fond memories of going up the hill behind my great-grandparent's home in coastal Oregon, learning to stalk, and listening to him talk about his philosophy of hunting. One shot to put the critter down. Two, if you had to. But three shots and you were a damn'fool who'd have been better to stay home. He couldn't abide someone who would take a shot if they weren't certain of their target. As you'll see from his stories, he was a skilled hunter, and one who hunted to make sure his family stayed fed. I have no idea what he'd have thought of this book, or of the great-granddaughter who came to pull it together, but I hope he'd be pleased. He had a prodigious sense of humor.

The other thing this project let me do was really dwell on the generational aspect of hunting. You'll find the final story in this volume reflects on that, and I don't know about you, but the room was a bit dusty when I read it. In illustrating this book, and the volume before it, I've drawn my Grandpa Ron, my great-Grandma Ella, and my Great-Grandpa Vanderburg. They, along with my Grandma La Vaughn, passed down skills and stories to me, and I've failed to pass much along to my children. I did teach my eldest to hunt, and attempted to teach all of them to fish, but perhaps I need to make time before it's too late to teach more.

As you read these stories, you'll find that you laugh, and you will think about the creatures we once interacted with in ways a city-dweller doesn't appreciate: from the first story where a reluctant shot was made when a critter got to be a pest. We don't always hunt from a sense of need. Sometimes we hunt, as in L A Behm's story, out of the need to keep a population in check. Hunters are, and have been if they were in tune with the world around them, conservationists. Putting the world in balance is part of the role of the hunter.

Ultimately, it's about people. People who do right, who do wrong, and the human desire to survive, and when that's accomplished, to kick back and laugh about it. We tell stories around the campfire, and when we do there are generations speaking with us and through us.

I hope you enjoy this book, and that it reminds you of where we came from,

Cheers!

Cedar Sanderson

Editor, Illustrator, Publisher

Cedar

❦ 2 ❦

THE BEAR THAT CAME TO DINNER – AND STAYED BY LA VAUGHN KEMNOW

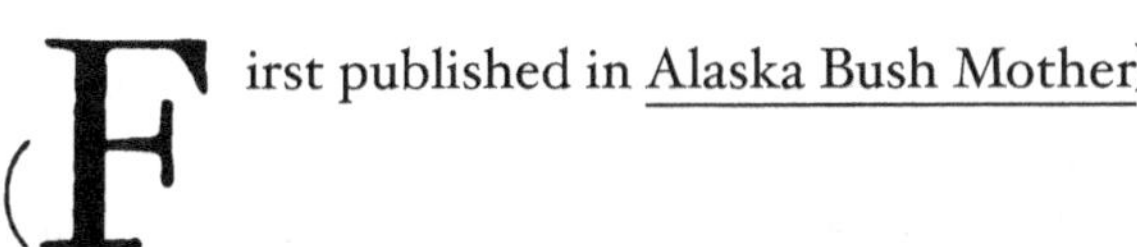

(First published in <u>Alaska Bush Mother</u>)

I WASN'T HUNTING BEAR – IT WAS MORE LIKE THE BEAR WAS HUNTING me!

I had just taken two rhubarb pies out of the oven, filling the Alaskan homestead cabin with tantalizing aromas; and was standing in the kitchen making out six loaves of bread to go in the oven later.

Catching movement from the corner of my eye, I turned my head to glance out the window. There was a medium-sized black bear standing up, facing the outhouse and raking its claws down the length of the black tarpaper that had been applied to keep the wind and winter snow from whistling through the cracks between the boards. It didn't worry me – the bear was outside and I was in the cabin with the doors shut.

Suddenly the bear dropped to the ground, whirled, and headed toward the corner of the cabin nearest the kitchen window. I hadn't known that a bear could move so fast! I had always thought of bears as being rather sluggish; how wrong I was!

The two little boys were sound asleep, having their naps. But six-year-old Kathy was awake and playing happily on a bed in a corner of the room. I thought *educational experience*, and called to Kathy to go to the window at the side of the room and she would see a bear going past.

She jumped off the bed, ran to the window, and let out a blood-curdling scream.

"He's right here, he's right here at the window!" she said as she fairly flew back onto the bed and cowered there in the corner. When she had gotten to the window, the bear's nose was on the other side, about six inches from Kathy's nose.

I had been calm about the whole thing, but her scream shook me up. I hastily turned and took the .30 carbine from over the kitchen door where it rested, ready for just such an emergency. As the bear made its way around the cabin, standing up at every window, sniffing at cracked panes of glass, picking up the aroma of the pies, I kept the rifle pointed in its direction.

I didn't want to shoot it; I just wanted it to go away.

The bear checked out each window in turn, scratched at the screens that covered some of them, and spent a minute or so batting at an old oil lantern that hung from the eaves. He spent several minutes snuffling around the kitchen door, then started pushing at it with a front paw.

This was a frightening turn of events. It was a heavy door made of slabs from the sawmill, but had a very light metal latch with a pull string —which often didn't latch and might have been easily pushed open.

I was scared. My breathing became labored. From six feet away I kept the rifle trained on the lower part of the door. If the bear had pushed it open, I was prepared to shoot.

I briefly considered shooting though the door, but was pretty sure that I would just wound him—which would make him very angry—so I didn't attempt that. Then the bear moved swiftly to the kitchen window, stood up and looked in at me, sniffing once more at cracked panes of glass.

He really wanted those rhubarb pies!

By that time my heart was starting to pound, my stomach was tightening with fear, and I was getting short of breath. Why wouldn't that bear just go away?

I was a little more than six months pregnant. I began to experience contractions in my lower abdomen. I felt faint—I visualized myself unconscious on the floor, the bear smashing a window, coming in, ripping open my belly, and eating my baby.

I made a decision. As the bear stood once more at the window opposite the kitchen, with great thick slobbers running down the glass, I stood in the center of the room and took careful aim. The end of the gun barrel was about eight feet from the bear's snout.

I fired.

The bullet made a neat round hole in the small window pane, with cracks radiating out to the wooden window frame, and the bear went down

He was down but not out. He kept trying to get up, and falling back. I hadn't wanted to shoot him in the first place, and certainly didn't want a wounded bear in the woods. I stepped close to the window and shot him once more, through a lower window pane when he was down on the ground. This time he stayed down.

When I made the second shot, with the business end of the gun almost against the window pane, the glass imploded. Long thin shards of glass flew into the cabin like missiles, around me and over the bed, surrounding my little daughter.

Fortunately, neither of us was hurt.

I realized then that I should have knocked out the glass with the gun barrel before I shot.

For the rest of the afternoon, I experienced moderately severe abdominal contractions. Was I going to give birth nearly three months early? That was a frightening possibility with no one there to get help for me.

By the next morning the pains had subsided.

Later my grandfather in Oregon, who had a droll sense of humor, predicted that since I had been scared by a bear, my baby would be born with "bare" feet. (It was not until two months later that I learned I was carrying not one, but two babies. And sure enough, they were both born with bare feet!)

While this was the first black bear incident in Alaska that summer that I knew of at the time, there were more later. A couple of days after my bear had come to visit, I heard that another pregnant young woman in the Delta Junction area experienced the terror of having a bear trying to get into the cabin where she was living. The story, as I heard it, was that there was a gun in the cabin but she didn't know how to use it. She did have a telephone, though. She phoned someone, then hid in a closet until some men came and shot the bear.

The bears in Interior Alaska, for the most part, do not depend on fish for their sustenance. They feed largely on berries. The berry crop that year was late, and very scant, so the bears were hungry. Although attacks by black bears are considered to be rare, throughout the summer I heard several accounts of people being attacked by black bears, resulting in three deaths and several injuries, in separate incidents.

When the Game Warden came out to get the one I shot (a three-year-old male), he said that was the eighth bear in the area that he had been called out to pick up. I couldn't keep it because I had not yet purchased my hunting license for the year. I didn't want to keep it anyway; the bear was in poor condition and the meat wouldn't have been very good, and a summer pelt would have been poor also.

I would not want to repeat the experience!

DROP SEATS—HUNTER STYLE
BY WARREN VANDERBURG

Most everyone is called, one way or the other. Sometimes it is a call to breakfast, or perhaps we are called some bad names, but one—sometimes referred to as a call of nature—is among the most urgent. I am still trying to think of a reason all three of us received such a call at the same time, just as we got to that big log.

Just as we all got our trousers down around our ankles and were in a most undignified position, we heard the unmistakable thud, thud, of a running deer, above us and coming downhill, fast, like they always ran when silent old Watch was on the trail.

Working as though we were all tied up by the same string, we jumped up and pulled our pants up above our knees, then propped them there so we could stand, and move a little. I grabbed my .44 six-gun just as the deer—a spike—came out in sight and jumped the end of the log close to Norman.

He had grabbed his rifle and was hitching around trying to keep in a position to shoot without tripping on his britches, and then his .44 carbine belched fire. It was still too dark to see our sights, and dark enough so his short-barreled rifle was spouting flame like the fizzle end of a blow torch. As Norman turned on the log, a steady stream of fire seemed to be pouring out of the little Winchester.

When the buck got far enough downhill so I could shoot without glancing a bullet too close to Norm, my .44 Colt joined the act. It was spouting flame out the barrel and also some was coming out between the cylinder and back end of the barrel.

And what was Ralph, the best shot among us, doing? He hadn't even picked up his rifle, but had his pants propped up with his knees, holding onto his middle with both hands, and laughing so hard he could hardly stand.

Just before the spike reached the foot of the hill and leveled out on the bench, Ralph managed to gasp to Norman, "He's hit. I see his tail going around in circles. Stop the dog." Then he was off on another laughing jag.

Well, Norm managed to catch Watch, we finished our rest stop and then sat on the log till it got light enough to shoot with sights—then Ralph took the dog and went alone after the deer. Watch slow-trailed it to where it had lain down. The spike jumped up and started to run, and Ralph broke its neck the first shot. (Norman had hit it once, put a bullet between the spike's hind legs as he ran straight away. All I hit was the ground.)

❧ 4 ❧
THE DOWNSIDE TO DOGS BY
L.A. BEHM II

Hunting stories are usually light and friendly. This one isn't. You've been warned.

I grew up hunting, fishing and camping. I joke with folks that I'm a simple country boy unaccustomed to their big city ways — when we left Waco in 1985, the population was north of 110,000 people. Not a small town in any way, shape or form.

Even in the 1980's, Texas had two real problems — feral hogs and feral dogs. Now, feral hogs are a real pain in the backside — they're destructive, and angry about it. They're also hard to kill from the wrong angle. You go into it knowing that if you stumble across feral hogs while wandering the wilds of Texas they are going to do their best to fuck you up. Well, unless you're two of my classmates from college who rented a place out in the middle of nowhere between San Marcos and Wimberly that they had permission from the owner to wander looking for archeological sites. I asked them what their plans were for hogs. They were shocked to learn that when Porky goes feral, he's no longer that nice little pink pig on the pork packaging.

Dogs, on the other hand, you know are going to be nice and friendly. Well, unless they're foaming at the mouth like Ol' Yeller, right?

Yeah . . . about that . . .

In my experience, there's two kinds of dogs you run across when you're out wandering the woods – farm dogs – they'll usually look like someone is taking care of them, have a collar, and not be total assholes.

The second type? Dogs that some human jackass has dumped that have survived to go feral. They're usually running in packs, look like hell, and ain't got time for you, human.

It's the second type we'll be talking about in a bit.

I graduated from the same college, twice. Two BA's. While I was in San Marcos the first time, I hung out with some like minded folk, and we'd go hunting during the season. Usually at least one dove hunt a year – which were usually excuses to take out every firearm we had ammo for and burn ammo – I mean have you ever tried to hunt dove? Little fraggers are damn hard to hit. I swear, they pump the wings twice, then fall until they realize they're about to hit the ground and pump the wings twice, repeat.

The 'Burn Ammo' hunt? That was the one we'd also check the deer stands on. Why? Because things grow up in front of them, so you've got to clear the sight lines. Things – usually things with far too many legs – also like to move into these nice, weather proof shelters that the humans build to hunt out of it, and the time to sweep for wasps and clear the lines of site is not at oh my god its early in the morning on opening day when you're probably going to miss the shot at that ENORMOUS BUCK with the HUUUUGEEE RACK! You know, the one that your grandfather and father both missed the shot at because there was a tree growing right there that wasn't there a week ago, I swear.

Anyway, we're wandering through the woods, checking the deer stands; there's five of us, see? Me, Carl, his brother John, The Guy Who's Name I Can't Remember (TGWNICR) and Carl's Girlfriend (CG), who was seriously carbonating my hormones – which is beside the point, but I've always had a thing for women who are at home gutting deer and cleaning birds. We looked like we were ready for the zombie apocalypse. In addition to shotguns, pistols and load bearing equipment, we were carrying machetes, axes, at least one chain saw, and implements of destruction and were walking down the cow trails to the various deer stands on the property.

You've never heard of cow trails? Ranch cows on a property that is allowed to go 'natural' will wear trails in what I've always referred to as Central to South Texas foliate jungle – huge, tangled masses of vines, usually green briar, juniper and mesquite trees. Course, if it weren't for the cows, the mesquite wouldn't spread as well. You can tell a cow trail from a deer trail by the width – if the trail is narrow and twisting with the underbrush tight on the sides, it's a deer trail. If, on the other hand, the underbrush is short in close, and then rounds out away from the base of the trail, it's a cow trail. Used to tell my brother stories about the trail blazing Daniel Cow, who wandered across ranches blazing trails for other cows to follow.

He'd ask how they knew which ones to follow.

And I'd reply they follow the bullshit, of course. . .

We're walking along and come up on the next stand. This was the 'long range' stand, according to John. It was along the property line and faced out over a small to medium sized meadow.

Which was the current residence of a pack of feral dogs.

We look at the dogs. They look at us. We give each other looks out of the corner of our eyes. Carl reaches down and grabs a rock and tosses it in the general direction of the dogs.

Wanna know how you can tell a dog is feral as opposed to wild? Yeet a rock at it. A wild dog – one that is born in the wild, raised in a pack, etc – will take off running nine times out of ten. Feral dog – one that some human bunghole dropped off in the wild because it's a dog and it can take care of itself – will look at you. Oh, it might move off a couple of feet, but it knows, deep in it's doggy heart that the human isn't going to do anything. It's been around humans.

These were feral dogs. They looked at us and started growling. We'd invaded their space, after all.

Remember when I said feral hogs are destructive? Feral dogs are too. And worse, we'd had several warm winters in a row, so there were . . . issues shall we say . . . with rabies in that part of the state. We hadn't quite reached the 'air dropping rabies vaccine laced bait' or the far more serious 'air dropping poisoned bait' to resolve the issue, but we were close – in the next six years 15 of the 17 human cases of rabies would be in Texas.

"We should just back off," TGWNICR said.

"Good plan," Carl agreed.

We started back down the trail – we could check the stand later.

The dogs followed. We tried a couple more stones. No good. They ignored them.

One of them charged, growling. We did the only thing we could do at that point – I love dogs, but I've got the scars to prove I've been bitten by more than one of them.

Having to kill the dogs wasn't the worst part. We were conscientious about it. We dragged all the dogs we shot back to the truck. This was in the pre-cell phone days. TGWNICR jumped in his blazer with John and took off to find a phone so we could call Texas Department of Health and get the remains tested.

❋ 5 ❋

THE TURKEY HUNT THAT
WASN'T BY DR LATEBLOOMER

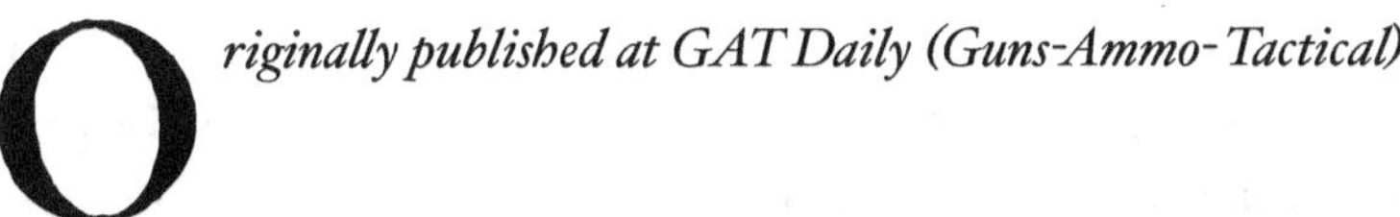

riginally published at GAT Daily (Guns-Ammo-Tactical)

I WANT TO TELL YOU A STORY ABOUT MY SECOND TURKEY HUNT. NOT the first one – which was a great experience with a mentor this spring, and unique in it's own way – but the SECOND experience. Because the second experience is a better story. I'm telling you a story, because I didn't shoot a turkey to brag about. A story is all I've got.

First, I have to make a bunch of excuses. Sometimes life just gets in the way. This spring was my very first attempt at a turkey season of any kind. But I also had three numb fingers due to carpal tunnel issues and had to have hand surgery because I was getting progressive nerve damage. The opening day of Spring Gobbler Season found me still with sutures in place from surgery earlier in the month. Though it was my left hand and not my trigger hand, I didn't think that the tender sutured palm was going to hold up to supporting a shotgun in the field. Not to mention that I had very little grip strength in that hand. So that screwed the first weekend of the season, and I stayed home.

The following weekend, with the sutures removed, I WAS able to get out with my mentor and friend for a morning hunt to at least get a taste of things. We heard a few distant gobbles, but were not able to convince any Toms to come closer. The experience DID whet my appetite though, I learned a lot, and it was a fun first experience.

The weekend after that my Mother was ill, so that Saturday was spent visiting her for Mother's Day instead of afield. I was also on-call.

The next available weekday forecast promised severe thunderstorms and quarter-size hail, so I stayed home yet again as I anxiously watched the season tick by. I contented myself with making cosmetic modifications to my shotgun, so that did help my attitude a little.

The NEXT available Saturday forecast promised heavy rain. There was due to be a few hours break in between storms, so I invited my adult daughter to come with me to check how the camera and blind had fared in the hail storm. Naturally, because I had not brought hunting gear, the weather cleared in late morning and stayed clear. Figures.

We did flush a turkey on the path through the woods though. I was armed with only a .357 and not a 12 gauge, so I simply watched as the turkey noisily broke cover and ascended on heavy wings up over the tree tops, and out of sight. I did yell "BANG" at it though, just to make myself feel better.

The following weekend was Memorial Day Weekend and my LAST opportunity to act as if I really were a turkey hunter. There is no Sunday hunting in that state, so Saturday was my big opportunity, and is where my second hunt story begins.

The property is over two hours away. It takes a bit of pre-planning to hunt up there, especially if you want to be there before dawn. When I got home from work that Friday evening, I was exhausted. I was also on-call again, but it was the last weekend of the season, so I thought I'd chance it. I didn't want to overpay for a hotel up there on a holiday weekend just so that I could already be there in the morning. But I was too tired to load up the gear and sleep overnight in the car. So I packed a cooler-ready picnic lunch, pre-loaded the Subaru, and went to bed early.

The alarm went off at 3:30 AM. Yeah, that was my reaction too. I did manage to slowly drag my sorry butt out of bed, but it was ugly. To say I was moving slowly would be an understatement. I think I felt every joint in my body creak. Despite my best intentions and a cooperative coffee pot, I didn't leave the house until after 5 AM – which got me to the property gate about 7:30 AM. Obviously well after dawn. Not an auspicious beginning.

On the road to the gate, I met a ruffed grouse. While it was in fact a grouse, it did its best imitation of a squirrel, as it darted into the road, stopped in the middle, feinted as if to go right, then took a few steps left, and stopped in the middle again. I was forced to bring the car to a full stop while the bird made up its mind. In retrospect, this little tableau was a foreshadowing of my whole morning.

After Mr. or Ms. Grouse made it safely to the side of the road, I unlocked the gate, pulled the car into the clearing and popped the back hatch. I decided to walk the half-mile or so through the woods to the spot I wanted to go, so I hitched on my Walmart Turkey vest, made sure I had calls and shells and a water bottle (the temp was already over 70 degrees), shouldered the gun and away I went. Except a couple hundred yards down into the woods I realized that I had forgotten Henrietta the Decoy.

Heaving a sigh, I trudged back up to the car, flung the bag containing Henrietta over my shoulder and started back again. I was already breaking a sweat in my full body camo and I hadn't even gotten started. When I closed the hatch, I could have sworn I heard a gobble in the far distance behind me, but "behind me" was way off the property. It turns out that was the only gobble I heard all day.

I took my time quietly working my way down the path through the trees, noting with annoyance that there were new ATV tire tracks in the mud since the previous week. A pox on teenagers with ATVs. I understand that the machines are useful as farm equipment and as often necessary transportation when setting up a blind or hauling out a harvested deer. But I absolutely cannot abide trespassing joyriders tearing up the landscape.

It had rained overnight. In truth it had barely stopped raining all month – there were literally tadpoles in the mud puddles for crying out loud. My trip down the path was accompanied by the sound of water dropping off the leaves of the trees, and the "Bung-glung" of a bullfrog over in the marsh. The birds were busy with their morning jabber while the mist started rising into the sunshine. If nothing else, it was a beautiful morning.

As I approached the meadow along the muddy access road, I heard a noise I hadn't heard up there before. There was a whooshing noise coming from the gas well across the meadow. Approaching cautiously, I ascertained that the noise was indeed coming from the well equipment, and decided that I'd better call the gas company guy.

That was phone call number one. I left a voice mail, but decided not to stick around too close, in case there was really something seriously wrong. I worked my way back down the road to a spot under a pine tree that looked promising, and seemed a safe enough distance away from the well. About ten minutes later my phone buzzed on my belt. It was the well guy calling back. He said he'd be there in about 20 minutes. That was phone call number two.

I had tried my slate call a few times during all of this, but had gotten no response. While I peeked over the weeds and wondered whether this day was going to get any better, I heard engines revving in the distance. The sound got closer until I saw two ATV's emerging from the trees on the access road coming toward me. Now I was mad. I stood up from my hiding place and strode over to the dirt road – still in full body camo, with my 12 ga in the crook of my arm – and stood there waiting for them. I pointed to the spot in front of me, indicating that I wanted them to stop.

"This is private property, guys", I announced to the two young men, over the noise of their infernal machines.

"Oh, we're sorry ma'am, we didn't see any signs." Which I knew was a lie, because I'd been posting for two months, but I let it slide. "You won't see us back here again" they assured me.

They were polite, but I'll believe it when I don't see them again. I advised them to turn around and go back the way they came, as I didn't have a key to the upper gate. At least they did as I requested. By the time I sat back down under my tree, I was all stirred up. Hopefully word will gradually get around that this isn't an absentee owner property anymore, and the signs mean what they say.

Ten minutes after that little episode, the gas well guy arrived in his pick-up. He grabbed a big wrench and made some adjustments which made the whooshing stop. It turns out that I wasn't just being paranoid after all – there was a legit pressure problem – and he thanked me for calling.

Five minutes after the well guy left, my phone buzzed on my belt again. I was being paged with a baby formula question. That was phone call number three. *Sigh* – Three strikes and you're out. I gave up on getting any hunting done that day. I figured no self-respecting turkey would be within miles of my location after all of that activity, and I might as well just pack it in. What a cluster.

I was pretty disgusted with myself and the situation by that point and was not at all quiet or careful on my walk back to the car, so naturally I kicked out a hen on my way back through the woods.

That has been the really frustrating thing. There ARE turkeys there. The tracks are all over the place in the mud puddles in the road, and I caught several of them on trail cam. I just didn't manage to have a gobbler show up when I had a shotgun in my hands. And honestly, I really don't have enough experience to know what I'm doing yet.

When I got back to the car I was in a pretty foul mood. I stripped off my gear, hopped up into the back and tucked into my lunch from the cooler. As I was chewing, a THIRD ATV trespasser showed up. He saw me hop down from my tailgate, and probably saw the .357 on my hip, because he didn't even have the courtesy to stop and talk to me. He just turned around and headed back out to the main road. There IS a locked gate, but the damned ATVers have created their own off-road entrances, so it's not like they don't know this is private property – they just don't care. That's the part that really bunches my bloomers.

So, my first attempt at a solo turkey hunt without a mentor was a complete cluster. With all of that drama, I was both cranked-up and let-down all at the same time. I just felt defeated. My season – that I had worked so hard for and so eagerly anticipated – was over.

I brooded over it for a while, but I finally realized that I was looking at the situation all wrong. When viewed in a different light, although my game bag was empty, I was still a fair badass.

I did months-worth of turkey learning, cam scouting, and property hiking on my own. Then with only one day of working with a mentor under my belt, and dealing with a post-op gimp hand, I was willing to at least TRY to venture out by myself. I got my own sorry butt out of bed at an ungodly hour and drove my own durn self two-plus hours to a different state. I humped my own gear to the hunt location, found a problem when I got there, addressed that problem, and still continued to try to hunt. I dealt with each new issue as it arose, and even handled not just one, not just two, but three trespassers all by my own self as a frumpy middle-aged woman alone. And to top it off, I had packed my own homemade lunch with homemade bread, homemade beef jerky and homemade fruit leather. If all that doesn't earn me at least a self-sufficiency badge and a modicum of self-pride, I don't know what would.

So, that's my story, and I'm sticking to it. I'm disappointed but I'll get over it. I've got the whole summer now to camp-out and pattern deer (I already found a bunch of trails and caught a young buck in velvet on cam), and I hear there's such a thing as Fall Turkey Season. Hmmm, I wonder what THAT's like ...

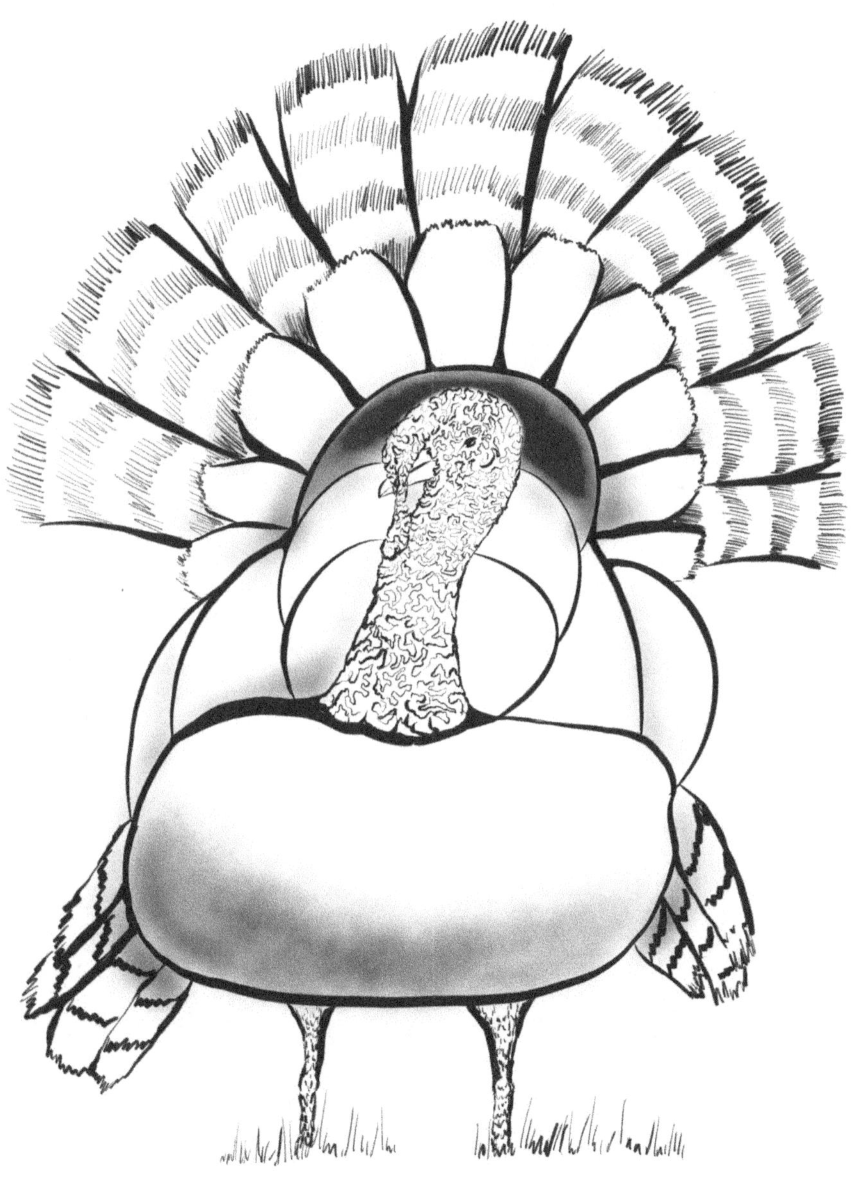

6

PRIMITIVE WEAPONS, MODERN PROBLEMS BY NIKO DEPOFI

Roughly thirty years ago, give or take a few years, I remember hunting with my father in Pennsylvania, when I was too young to hold a PA hunting license.I would follow him around in layer after layer of second-hand winter clothes, with an orange vest thrown on top for safety, as he hunted Pennsylvania State Game Lands for whitetail deer and/or turkey.

One trip stands out as uniquely humorous: we had spent a very cold, snowy morning hunting somewhere near the Allegheny mountains, several hours from our home, and Dad had seen and shot at several deer in that time. Now, my father isn't a target shooter, but usually when he is hunting, he doesn't miss.He has an entire house full of photographs and mounts, and we've eaten everything over the years, to prove that he is a capable hunter and competent with a firearm.

This day, he missed. Several times. One was a good-sized buck.

Now Dad has a temper, everybody in my family does really, and when I was a wee lad, I knew better than to 'mouth off' when he was in a mood. Missing several deer while hunting in a near-blizzard was really getting on his nerves, so I was being quiet and just holding still when he told me to, but I noticed something after his last missed shot.At the time, Pennsylvania was very strict in its primitive weapons season, requiring a flintlock, cloth patches, traditional sights, and round ball ammunition. Looking at Pennsylvania's Muzzleloader regulations now, this is no longer the case.

In those years, my family did everything we possibly could ourselves. We grew a large garden with carrots, zucchini, potatoes, tomatoes, lettuce, several types of beans, peas, cabbage, broccoli and cauliflower, corn, pumpkin, onions, garlic, cayenne peppers, everything we could get to grow. We picked our own blackberries, raspberries, elderberries, apples, cherries, and strawberries, we canned it all, and we hunted and fished to fill our freezers.

People who rant against hunting have never had to rely on it for dinner.

This self-sufficiency included fletching our own arrows and casting our own round ball (for Pennsylvania) and mini-ball ammunition for our muzzleloaders. We had several molds and frequently melted down old fishing sinkers or tire weights for lead. (If you've never spent an afternoon along a country highway looking for tire weights that have fallen off, count yourself lucky.) The resulting lead would be skimmed to remove impurities that floated to the top, then poured into a hand mold that looked like a pair of pliers with a long, two-piece metal clamp instead of jaws. Wait a few minutes, open the mold and you have several round balls or mini balls for muzzleloaders. We also had fishing jig molds as well.

I watched as my father reloaded his flintlock, the butt stock seated on the top of his boot to keep it out of the snow, the brass-and-wood ramrod tap-tap-tapping the round ball and linen patch down into the FFF black powder. I was worried, you see, since Dad was already in a foul mood, that I would be asked to do something and not notice, or that I would do something I shouldn't. Then, as Dad made himself ready to move to a new spot, he put the buttstock of the rifle under his armpit, I heard a soft 'thupt' sound. Looking down, I saw an odd hole in the snow.

I used my hand to scoop up some snow, and also found a round piece of lead.

"Dad, I think the shot just fell out," I said, quietly. He turned and looked at me with a puzzled look on his face. I handed him the round ball, which he looked at for a moment before wiping it dry on his handkerchief, then placing it in the barrel of the .45 caliber muzzleloader. Tilting the rifle back, we both heard it roll down the barrel, and neither of us heard it hit anything that would sound like a piece of lead when it hit bottom. My father tilted the barrel back down, and out rolled the round ball into the snow.

Just to be certain, he primed the pan, cocked the hammer back, and shot the muzzle loader at a dead tree stump thirty feet away or so, a great big pine stump with snow all over it. There would be no way to miss it or miss the impact from the shot. FIZZZ-FWOMP! The muzzleloader fired, but the sound wasn't even right, now that we were listening carefully. Sure enough, nothing but smoke and the burning patch came out of that long rifle.

Nothing happened for a moment, and then my father started to laugh. We picked up the pace and headed back to the truck, all the round ball he had with him was from the same bullet mold, and all the patches were cotton ticking, pre-cut with a piece of pipe we had sharpened into a small punch that could be hammered through layers of cloth easily, none of which would help if the round ball wasn't the right size. The bullet mold was defective, producing shot that was far too small.

My father had been firing blanks at the deer of Pennsylvania all morning without knowing it.

(And he still laughs when I tell this story, too...)

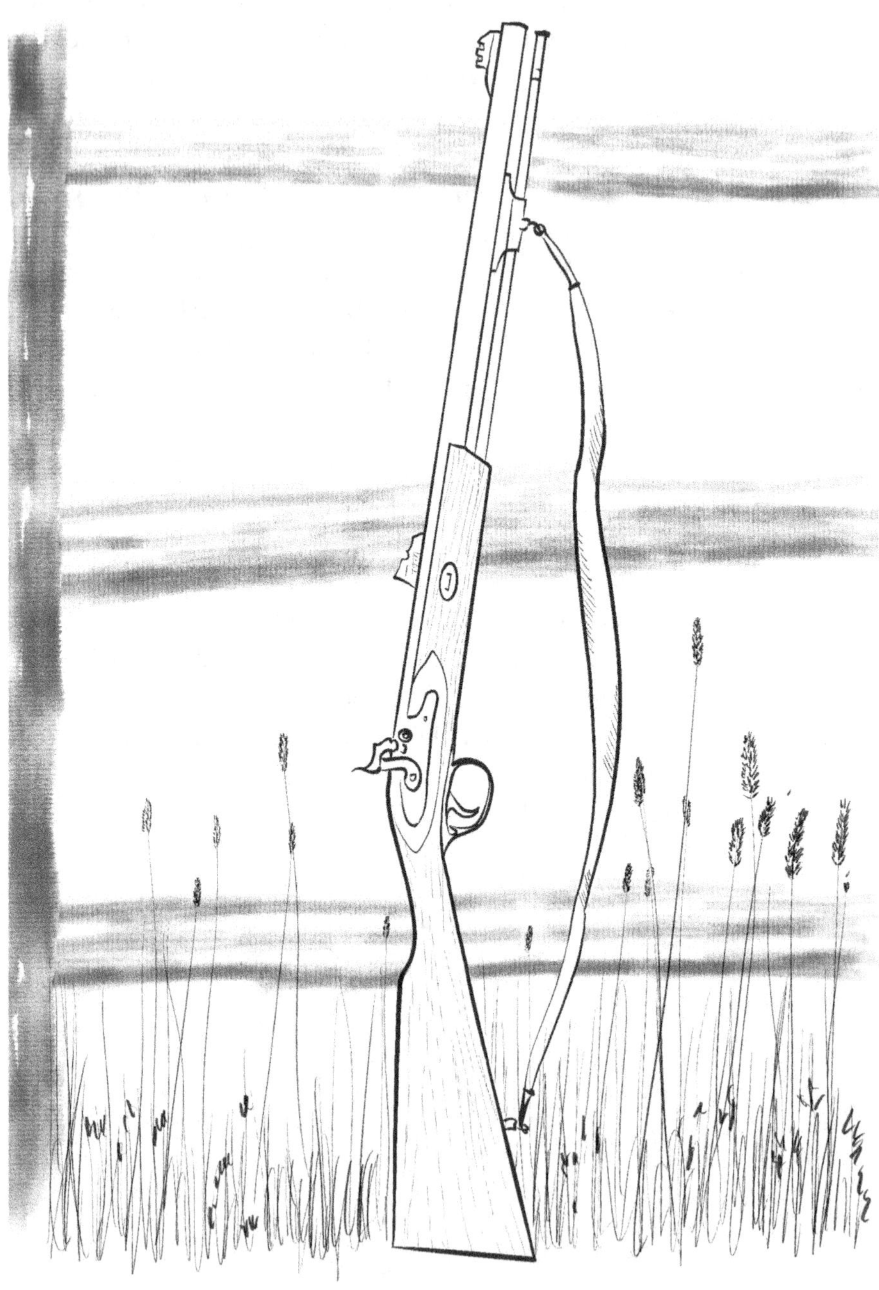

7

A HUNTING TRIP BY DOUG IRVIN

My friends and I had a tradition. The weekend after Thanksgiving – the opening of Hunting Season – we'd spend the long weekend on a hunting and camping trip.

It was a chance to return to nature; to prove that modern trappings aside, we could reconnect with our cave men ancestors and prove that we had what it took. We lacked only mastodons as our prey.

So as last Thanksgiving approached, we made of plans. Then things took a twist.

My wife, Edith, confronted me.

"I want to go", she said stubbornly. I guess she knew there would be an argument.

"Edith," I reasoned. "You can't go. One woman among half a dozen men? That's not even reasonable. I mean, most of the guys are pretty civilized, but a couple tend to take the caveman attitude seriously."

"So you think I'd be in personal danger," she remarked candidly. Okay, that was hazardous ground. Edith had taken martial arts from the time she entered grade school, and she had more colored Belts than most women had shoes. I wasn't scared of sleeping on the couch, or in the dog house. I feared how I would arrive there. And what velocity I would achieve.

"Well, no. The guys all know you. But this is guy time. Time to snort and spit and belch. And other rude noises."

"I'm married to you. We have a teen-age son, who has other teen aged boys as friends. What do you think will shock me?"

I couldn't answer that. Finally, in desperation I told her I'd present it to the guys. If they were all agreeable, one hundred percent, she could go.

The traitors backstabbed me!

Alex, my long time from middle school buddy, decided we needed to be reasonable.

"Besides," he remarked, "once Edith sees how rough it is, the other wives will beg off any invites. We'll be safe." The others agreed.

So, the Friday after Thanksgiving we set off, real early. Oh-Dark-Thirty early. Even so, Edith made sure we had a substantial breakfast to arm us for the trip. Bacon. Eggs. Biscuits. Gravy! I almost went back for seconds, but the guys were tapping their horns at the street for us to get a move on. The truck was packed the night before, so all we needed to do was grab last minute items and take off.

The trip into the mountains took a bit over four hours to reach our usual camp spot. Once there, we set up tents and put in a camp fire spot for when we returned. All we'd need to do was start the fire, then wait for the coals to form for cooking.

Edith chose to stay in camp. Thankfully. I was sure she'd want to go out with me, and maybe talk and scare off the deer.

About the time the sun started dipping towards the horizon, I packed up and headed for camp. I never count on getting a shot the first day. And besides, a mid-afternoon lunch of snackables and granola bars, washed down with tepid water, made me hungry for half-cooked meat seared over the open flames of our fire.

I wandered into camp about the same time a couple of other guys did. And met with a surprise.

Edith had made a thick stew, cooking it over the metal tripod we had over the fire pit. On the side, a large pot of coffee steamed, with cups stacked next to it. Several branches had toasted bread twists, browned and ready for eating. A metal bowl had butter waiting to be spread on them.

We dug in gratefully; glad we didn't have to wait a couple of hours for food. After dinner, Edith collected all the dirty bowls and utensils, washed them in hot water she had simmering by the fire, and took herself off. I suppose sometime or another she went to our tent to bed down. At least she was there when I finally turned in, after an evening of jaw-jacking and brags.

Next morning, she was up before I woke, and out of the tent. A pot of hot coffee waited us. And pancakes. Loads of pancakes and syrup and patty sausages.

And when we leaned back groaning in satisfaction, she handed each of us a bag. I peeked in mine. When did she have time to make biscuits? Inside each was a sausage patty, and a few restaurant style jelly packets. And a couple of bottles of fruit juices. Somehow, she knew each of our favorites.

"Be sure you bring back the trash, boys!" She called as we wandered, reluctantly from camp.

The second day of hunting was fairly successful, and a couple of us toted our kills back to camp after field dressing them.

Dinner that night was fresh venison steaks, steamed corn with butter, rolls, and lots of hot coffee. As the sun dropped behind the hills, Edith brought out a deep dish peach crisp. No ice cream, but she had thick cream to pour over the top.

Once again, after washing up, she left the campfire.

Sunday morning came along, our last day for camp, and the last chance for everyone to bag their deer. For some strange reason, Edith wasn't in camp. But we hardly noticed as fresh biscuits, creamy gravy, and lots of coffee was ready for us. We planned on returning to camp around noon, clean things up and pack out the camp. We picked up our individual lunch bags, shouldered our rifles, and headed out.

When we got back to camp just as the sun made it to the top of the sky, everything was broke down and ready to be packed up. And Edith had a big Muley deer hung up from a tree and cleaned out. We gladly loaded her kill in the cold trailer, then headed for the road home.

Somehow, all the horrors we expected from having a woman along never appeared.

The next year, right before Thanksgiving, I had an attack of acute appendicitis, and was told sternly by my doctor that NO! I couldn't go hunting this year.

The guys came over to our home to meet for planning, and I had to sadly tell them I'd have to skip this year. They all shook their head sadly, then gave covert looks at each other.

Alex spoke up after looking at each of the others.

"Awfully sorry you have to miss out, guy." Then came the shocker.

"Can ... can Edith come?"

I didn't go hunting for a while after that.

❧ 8 ❧

NIGHT HUNT BY KAREN MYERS

Those old-timers George used to hunt with, they knew about costs, what it was to make choices. He thought of them as old-timers but they weren't, not really. Sure, some of them were classic "ridgies," mountain types, or their fathers were, or their grandfathers. They had small houses and cabins tucked into the hollows and blue collar jobs, fixing machinery, cutting wood, clearing brush — whatever they could do to make a living and still leave time for other pleasures, especially hunting and fishing. Most were in their fifties or much older. It was hard to tell sometimes — the life they led could be hard on a man. They were lean men, by and large, though here and there one ran to fat and was teased for it by the others.

Their wives and families lived quietly, and their children mostly moved away.

They weren't all like that, of course. Sometimes a more solid citizen in the community felt the urge to join them, an atavistic need to be a part of something else, something not modern and civilized. There were always a few like that, welcomed by the night hunters because they appreciated the fellow-feeling, and because these outsiders helped them keep things afloat when times turned tough, even got them work sometimes. Their fathers and their grandfathers had known each other for as long as they could remember.

He remembered the first time he'd met the night hunters. He'd wanted to see what it was like, chasing coon and fox in the dark with hounds. He'd read what he could about it, but there wasn't much — the people who did it and the people who wrote about it had very little overlap. He'd heard more, hints from friends who always seemed to have a couple of jars of moonshine on hand. He pestered one of them, Gabriel Scott, and one moonlit October night he was invited along. Gabe warned him, "Wear clothing you don't mind losing if it gets ripped to shreds."

The two of them drove deep back into a hollow around ten o'clock. Gabe took his pickup truck up the side of the Blue Ridge along a dirt road George had never traveled before. They pulled up at an old hunting cabin where half a dozen trucks were already settled, and ten or twelve men stood around an open fire. Some had one or two dogs on leashes by their side, and he saw others in kennels in the backs of the trucks.

He knew it was a sort of audition, and he conducted himself modestly, younger at twenty-seven than everyone there. He recognized a few of them by sight. Gabe introduced him as "that young fellow, George Traherne, who whips-in for the Rowanton Hunt. Gilbert Talbot's grandson. He knows foxhounds."

"Does he, now?" Lucius Conyngham drawled. His was a quiet, sardonic sort of voice, matched to a spare body that made no unnecessary movements. His battered old fedora hat looked well-accustomed to a life out of doors. George pegged him as the leader of the group.

"I want to know what it's like, sir, how you hunt," George said. "I'm here to learn."

That sparked a jeer from some, but a nod from Luke. "Alright, then." He walked among the men and passed their names to him. Most were friendly enough, preoccupied with catching up on the news and keeping their hounds out from underfoot. They bragged on their hounds to each other, boasting about how well they'd do this time.

Most of the men had one or another type of foxhound. George thought he recognized a couple of Walkers, and there were hounds that wouldn't have seemed out of place in any Virginia pack. Not all were foxhounds, however. One scowling fellow with black hair and scraggly eyebrows held a young lanky bluetick coonhound on a lead and was being joshed by his friends. "You brought him along again? Cain't you learn?"

Gabe told George, "Hank hasn't had much luck with his hound. Too slow to keep up with the others, and we hunt fox more than we do coon."

George knew it was a point of pride which hound ran the game best, who came closest, who treed the critter first, and how their voices sang in the night.

"We all here tonight?" Luke asked. The men stopped talking and looked around.

"Looks like," one of those by the fire said.

"Let's do 'er then." Luke walked over to his truck and released two redbones from their kennels, clipping leads onto their collars. More coonhounds, George thought in surprise. They whined with excitement, and all the hounds joined in.

He counted them in couples automatically, as if they were a pack of foxhounds. There were nine couple, eighteen hounds. A mixed pack, of course, both dogs and bitches. That young bluetick was one of the tallest.

Once they all had their hounds in hand, straining at their leads, Luke looked them over. "Let 'em loose," he said, and unclipped his two. They must have hunted with each other before, George thought, for they hung together like a pack and ghosted up the slope into the dark woods out of the firelight, seeking a scent trail.

The men settled down in a semicircle on the upwind side of the fire. There were plenty of log sections set upright for seats, and they sat quietly, listening for the first cry. Most of the leaves were already off the trees, up here on the ridge, so sound would carry well.

A quart jar of clear moonshine made the rounds. When it reached George he saw a piece of fruit inside, and he could taste the faint flavoring of the peach over the kick of the raw alcohol. He sipped and handed it along, listening to the men.

They spoke quietly. One had a son in the Marines and passed along the latest news. Another had a daughter who'd presented him with his first grandchildren, twin girls. There were chuckles at that, and congratulations raised to "grandpa" as the jar went by.

A great horned owl in the woods called out with its low hoots and they hushed to listen. It repeated itself once, then stopped. Just as they started to speak again, they heard the unearthly death shriek of a rabbit, probably the owl's victim. George shuddered, and the men around the fire were quick to resume talking, to shake off the gruesome sound.

One old fellow started a tale about his son who was pestering him to come live with him down on the flats, now that his wife had been gone for some time. "I told him I just wouldn't do it. I'm fine up here, I said, I ain't leaving. Not to no goddam suburb."

They shed their children to the modern world, but chose to stay themselves. He didn't know the man, but he could picture him ten years on, dying alone in his cabin. It wasn't a sad thought, exactly — he wanted the hard life for its joys and was willing to pay the cost. He could respect that.

Except for the trucks, you could almost believe this was another century, George thought. It's a world away from my job, shiny computers and corporate customers. He shook his daytime thoughts away and focused on the men around them, how well they fit together. He didn't romanticize it, even he could see they had factions among themselves, friends and cliques, but they were united in this love of hunting and that gave them a common bond that overrode their differences. He envied them.

A clear cry rang out, upslope and some distance away. All conversation ceased, and then the sound came again, with other voices supporting it. The hounds had struck on a hot scent. They listened for a few moments and Luke said, judiciously, "T'ain't no deer. I do believe that's gray fox. My Katie don't sound like that for coon. She's partial to fox."

A deep voice joined in. "Ain't that your hound, Hank?" one of the men asked.

"Yeah, but it's coon, not fox. You wait and see."

They don't agree, George thought, watching them hide their smiles. This is an old dispute between them.

Gabe told George, "Hank bought himself a coonhound and that's what he wants it to hunt. No use telling him different."

"I love his voice," George said. It was true. The deep baying set a foundation for the chorus of higher-pitched voices.

The sounds broke off, and the men hushed, waiting. In a few moments, they picked up again, coming toward them.

"Listen to that hound of Hank's bawl." The speaker shook his head in admiration.

"My Katie's in the lead, though." Luke said with quiet pride.

George sat, surrounded by dark woods and blinded by the fire, and tried to construct a picture to go with what he was hearing. The hounds were strung out, he could tell, the deep-voiced one trailing at the end and the clear voice of the first hound to sound off still in front. That must be Luke's Katie, he thought. The voices of eighteen hounds raised in joy and eagerness resounding down through the woods was uncanny. He remembered that Washington had received a gift of bluetick hounds from Lafayette and declared they sounded "like the bells of Moscow," Now he understood what that meant, here in the dark primeval forest of his imagination.

The pack swung away from them again and went quiet. One voice raised falteringly. "That's Rebel," one man said. They listened to the hounds working out the scent, each man identifying the voice of his own hounds and supplying commentary.

"I don't know what fouled the scent," a big, testy man said impatiently to his neighbor. "If that little Hazel of yours had any sense she'd stop working tail line and point the right way for a change."

"Quiet," Luke said, and they subsided. They picked up the line again and raised the full cry once more.

"That's more like it," Gabe said, and George nodded.

The baying changed its note, growing louder and more eager, and then it stopped moving, lighting up the mountainside with joyous noise.

"Alright, boys, on your feet," Luke said. "They've treed it."

They took out flashlights, all except for a couple of the men who picked up lanterns. Luke took the lead as they picked their way up the slope, moving as quickly as they could and cursing the bushes and branches that scratched at their clothing and the rocks that turned their ankles. George was larger than most and had a harder time pushing his way through, but he was young enough to make up for it and was determined not to be a fool and get left behind to wander lost for the rest of the night.

The lights weaving up ahead of him stopped and when he reached them he saw the hounds leaping at a beech tree that still clung to its tan leaves. The trunk leaned at an angle, and several of the hounds scrambled up a few feet, only to drop off defeated. The tall bluetick was among them, George saw, baying at the top of his lungs.

The men stood by their hounds and leashed them.

"Told you it was a coon," Hank crowed, as the flashlights probed through the leaves looking for the quarry.

The beams coalesced into a single spot, and George saw the pointed nose and grizzled muzzle of a gray fox, a dog fox, he thought, not a vixen. Secure in his perch, he looked down with unconcern at the hounds below. The hounds waited for the men to take a shot and deliver him.

"Goddam you, hound," Hank hollered. "That ain't no coon." He hauled the hound to him on its lead and gave it a good kick, then picked up the lead end and started to lash him with it. The frightened hound howled and pulled himself free. He fled, trailing his lead behind him, into the dark. The rest of the hounds quieted for a moment, startled.

The men froze at the unseemly outburst. No one said a word as Hank whined, to cover his action, "I paid four hundred dollars for that hound, and I'm done with him."

George spoke up for the first time that evening. "I'll give you four hundred for him. Right now." He reached into his wallet and pulled out everything he had on him, about three hundred and twenty dollars. He waved Gabe over. Gabe handed him his wallet without a word and he helped himself to another eighty. He walked over and threw the bills at Hank's feet. "There. He's mine now. You all heard him?" he asked, looking around the ring of silent men. They nodded, and he thought he saw approval on some of their faces.

Hank leaned over and picked up the money. "I ain't helping you catch him," he said. He laughed uneasily, not liking the mood of his companions, and started back down through the woods by himself.

Luke looked up at the fox and then back at the men whose celebration had soured. "I think we'll let this one off this time, boys, what do you say?"

They agreed and headed back with their leashed hounds, moving more slowly and carefully going down than they had scrambling up. George and Gabe lingered behind.

Gabe raised an eyebrow at him.

"I couldn't let him do that, and besides, I like that hound," George said.

"You're going to have to wait for him to find his way back once he gets over it," Gabe said. "Might as well go back to the fire. That's where he'll return. If he returns."

"I know, and it might take all night. You can go on, if you want, pick me up in the morning, maybe."

"Ah, hell, I haven't got anything better to do myself," Gabe said, and they pushed their way back down to the fire in companionable silence.

When they got there, they found Hank was gone. "What're you fixing to do with that hound, if he comes back?" Lucius Conyngham asked.

"There's more to life than night hunting," George said, "though maybe this isn't the crowd to say that to. And more than coming in first."

Luke let a small smile escape him.

"Well, you could be right, at that. Someone's got to be tail hound. And he surely did enjoy himself, bawling at that fox."

"Yes, sir, he surely did," George replied.

A different moonshine jar was pressed into his hand. This one had an apple inside. He took a sip and waited a moment to catch his breath, then passed it along to Luke.

"I think we're done for the night," Luke said. "You're welcome to join us another time, son. Gabe'll let you know." He touched the brim of his hat.

"Thank you, sir. I had a fine time in your company."

"Bring that hound, or not, as you like."

They bundled their hounds into their trucks and drove off, one at a time, leaving only Gabe's truck behind. The noise of the engines and the tires on the dirt road carried for a while in the still night, but gradually died away.

"He left us a gift," Gabe said, pointing to a half-filled jar. "Something to pass the time with."

They sat next to each other by the fire, sipping away, and pausing every now and then to throw another log on to keep it alive. "You won't see that Hank again," Gabe said. "No one treats a dog like that when he's just doing his job. They won't tolerate it."

They chatted about inconsequential things in the night and watched the moon drift slowly across the sky. After an hour or so had passed, Gabe said, "Think that fool hound has enough sense to work the back trail to find his way here?"

"Probably." Hounds mostly did make their way back to where they started from when they got lost. That's why hunters left a coat behind if they had to leave. Like as not, they'd find their hound sleeping on it in the morning.

"What're you going to name him?"

"Hugo, I think. Don't know why, just seems right."

Gabe grunted and reached for the jar.

George looked up and thought he saw movement. "Hssht. Don't move."

The bluetick came tentatively out of the woods and stood outside the firelight, watching them, whining softly.

"It's alright, boy," George said in a calm voice. "He's gone. Come on in."

He kept talking, soothing the hound and patting the side of his leg. The hound circled around the fire, taking a long sniff of the log where Hank had been sitting.

"Don't you think about him anymore," George said. "You come on over and get a fuss made over you. Such a fine hound, finding that fox with the others, staying on the trail and helping them tree it. You're a good hound, you are."

The sound of the low sweet-talking voice enticed the hound all the way in, and George rubbed him all over, getting him used to the feel of his hands. He'd treated dozens of foxhounds this way, over the years, and he knew how to make a hound feel at home. "Your name is Hugo, now, and you're going to live with me."

"You do have a way with them," Gabe said.

❀ *9* ❀

FORTYMILE CARIBOU BLUES
BY BRENNAN HANKINS

I enlisted in the Air Force in the spring of 2012. Prior to that, I had been doing a series of odd jobs in Oregon, my home, and Alaska, my home away from home. My dad's family, him included, is full of commercial fishermen, most of whom fish in Alaska, and at the time I enlisted, I was familiar with most of the southern coastal towns and the entire Kenai Peninsula south of Midtown Anchorage.

After basic training, and while I was in technical training, I was notified of the location of my first duty station: "Hankins, you're going to Alaska!"

Cue young Airman Me: "But I just came from there!"

But the Air Force had need of me up North, and so I was sent up for a three year tour in the Last Frontier.

Not that I was complaining, of course. Anchorage is the airport hub for the entire state of Alaska, and unless you're on a direct flight to Juneau or riding the Milk Run (which stops at every little town in Southeast between SeaTac International and Ted Stevens International Airport), if you're flying to any location in Alaska, you have to change planes at Ted Stevens—in Anchorage. This meant that any time I had relatives flying north for fishing season, I got to see them, and at least have lunch. That was pretty cool.

However, prior to getting stationed at Joint Base Elmendorf-Richardson, I had never been north of Northern Lights Boulevard, in Midtown Anchorage. Getting to spend three whole years up there (and not having to spend it on a fishing boat somewhere in the Gulf of Alaska, or Prince William Sound), meant I actually got the opportunity to explore the state quite a bit, an experience I am forever grateful for.

Cue Technical Sergeant John Honeysett.

TSgt Honeysett was my shop NCOIC (Non-Commissioned Officer In Charge) and my temporary supervisor when I first arrived to Elmendorf (my actual supervisor was deployed at the time). He quickly took me under his wing, and when it came time for caribou season, I was invited to tag along for a week-long trip over in the Fortymile Mining District, a three-hundred-plus mile drive southeast of Fairbanks.

The Fortymile area is about as remote as you can get. We were about thirty miles northwest of the Poker Creek Border Crossing (the northernmost land border crossing in North America, which provides direct road access from Alaska to Dawson City in Yukon Territory, Canada), and about a hundred and twenty miles northeast of Tok, the nearest town with year-round highway access, plumbing, and a power grid. The nearest town period is Chicken (Permanent Population: 12), so named because the founders couldn't agree on how to properly spell "ptarmigan" (true story). The road that leads to Fortymile, the Taylor Highway (Alaska State Highway 5), is paved for the first sixty miles (just shy of reaching Chicken) and only open in the summer; the highway goes all the way up to the towns of Eagle and Fort Yukon. Services are non-existent (save for a tiny gas station in front of the Chicken Mercantile Store and a few BLM campsites); folks desiring to head up that way ought to be prepared to rough it.

And prepared to rough it we were: four ATVs, two boxes of shells per firearm, tents, cooking implements, fuel cans, water cans, a little firewood, a little cooler full of sandwich fixings, chips, and canned goods, and a big, six-foot-long cooler filled to the brim with beer, for good measure. Because Alaska.

There was five of us: Preston, a retired technical sergeant working as a civilian in the Interior Electric Shop, Luke, a retired technical sergeant working in the Exterior Electric Shop (where TSgt Honeysett and I worked), Cole, an active duty technical sergeant and a friend of Luke's that worked in an Ammo squadron, TSgt Honeysett, and young Airman First Class me, the young buck of the group.

The trip to Fortymile had been long. I showed up late to TSgt Honeysett's house, he encountered issues with the trailer he bought to haul the wheelers with the entire way, all on top of an eight-and-a-half hour drive to where we would later disembark on wheelers to where we were going to set up camp.

Seven-and-a-half hours in, Sergeant Honeysett was leading the convoy (the other three were riding in Preston's truck), and he was getting pretty tired of driving. He reached into the backseat, popped open the big cooler, scooped a wobble pop of the "Milwaukee's Best" variety, and took a sip.

Cue, young, innocent me: "Sir, would you like me to drive?"

"Naw," he said, taking another sip, "Don't worry. This isn't my first booze cruise."

Welcome to Alaska.[1]

⚜

WE REACHED OUR JUMPING OFF POINT, JUST NORTHWEST OF JACK Wade Junction, the point where the Taylor Highway, which heads north to Eagle and Fort Yukon, splits off from the Top Of The World Highway, which leads to the Poker Creek Border Crossing and Dawson City. From there, we traveled up a mining road via ATVs to where we ended up setting up camp.

The mining road we came in on goes in an east/west direction, between the Taylor Highway and the Ulner Creek Mine. Eight miles in, this road crosses between a small Knoll to the south and a larger Mountain to the north. A two-track ATV trail crosses the mining road at this point; this two-track goes for a ways up the Mountain to the north, and peters out at the top of the Knoll to the south. This little hill overlooks a Draw at the top of a steep Valley to the southeast, which leads down to Ulner Creek, a small Slope overlooking this Valley to the east, and a big open Plain on a shelf to the west, all south of the mining road. This whole area had been ravaged by a lightning-sparked wildfire almost a decade earlier, leaving the immediate area around the hill a mess of dead timber and waist-high new growth; the result resembling a grassy Knoll with sight lines so perfect I'm pretty sure Lee Harvey Oswald popped a boner thinking about it.

The south side of this Knoll had a small Flat Spot on it, just below the Knoll's summit. That was where we set up Camp.

We arrived about a week ahead of the opener for the general caribou season (which ended up being only two days for our hunting unit) to scout the caribou herds, which was probably a good thing. See, in Alaska, it's legal to road hunt (or, at least it was at the time), provided said road is not a highway. When we arrived, nobody else was out there; we settled in and killed the week scouting for caribou, monitoring reports on herd movement from Fish & Game, doing a bit of sage grouse hunting (Luke and Preston both brought shotguns for the purpose), building a stand for dressing out any caribou we happened to get on the edge of the Camp Flat, whittling (which I took up enthusiastically), and getting absolutely knackered around the campfire at night.

The day prior to the opener, everybody and his brother was out there, to the point where it was nigh impossible for others to find a spot to set up a blind, and as a result, we saw many a douchebag blasting a dirt bike or side-by-side up and down the mining road, trying to catch caribou within sight of the road.

This was slightly understandable, though. The day before the opener, we had a herd of 40 caribou and change walk right through the middle of our camp like we weren't even there. I woke up that morning to see some absolutely gorgeous bulls in that pack, standing less than five feet from my tent.

You want to talk about testing of faith and character, there is no greater temptation than having a seven-point caribou standing in front of you at point blank range the day before the opener, and your rifle is loaded and within arm's reach. Fortunately, conscience and an extreme aversion to getting busted for poaching won out, and the herd left our camp unmolested.

By the by, for the uninitiated: In other parts of the world, the terms caribou and reindeer are used interchangeably, but in Alaska and Canada, there's a difference: Caribou are wild, reindeer are domesticated.

Hunting for reindeer is not the same thing as hunting for caribou. And if you're unfamiliar with what a caribou looks like, imagine a slightly larger deer, with a flat piece of antler, which is called a shovel, coming down off its rack and over its nose, flat sides exposed to port and starboard. Reindeer are identical, but, as they tend to be better fed (because domesticated), they tend to grow a little bigger.

Caribou tend to travel in big herds. The Fortymile Herd in particular tends to travel southeast in the spring towards the Interior Hills of the Yukon Territory, looking for forage. In the winter, they migrate northwest towards the northern end of the Tanana Valley, north of Delta Junction and Fairbanks. When migrating, if a threat is detected, caribou will either go around it or through it—but they will not turn around. My best guess as to why is, their navigational instinct is just that strong. And seeing the herds in action is nothing short of majestic.

Kinda reminds me of Kowalski in Vanishing Point, but with more antlers and less B-Body Mopar.

Back to the story.

After the herd cleared out, we started to devise a strategy. We had the whole of the Knoll to work with, as there was no practical way for other hunters to get to the hills between the top of the valley draw and the small plain to the west without walking directly through our camp. The caribou would follow a pattern, coming up the draw out of the valley and either skirting the Knoll to the south, between the Camp Flat and a slightly bigger hill directly to the south and circling back north around the Knoll on the Western Plain, or skirting the Knoll's Eastern Slope. Both of these migration routes would merge again on the northern side of the mining road, where the caribou would traverse the western side of the mountain and continue towards the northwest.

Preston had made a big show of wanting to be the first man to get a caribou. He claimed a spot on the hill to the south of us, looking down directly into the draw with a scoped .300 Winchester Magnum (WM) like he was ready to put Lyndon Bou Johnson into the Ungulate Oval Office. From there, on the western side of the Knoll overlooking the Plain, in order from south to north, was Cole (with a .270 WM rifle), TSgt Honeysett (with a .300 WM rifle and a 9MM concealed pistol) and Luke (with a .300 WM rifle). That left me and my grandpa's old Ruger

M77 .338 WM to myself on the east side, and based on the migration patterns we had been seeing, we'd figured that either Preston or I had the best chances of bagging a caribou. We spent the rest of the day before the opener using Luke's range finder to mark out distances with flagging tape, hit the hay early, and took up positions right before dawn broke.

Fast forward to roughly 0900 hours.

A small pack of roughly 12 caribou, three of them bulls, came up the top of the draw towards the south. I couldn't see them from my position, but Preston had a bird's eye view of them all. He dropped the lead bull like it was a Kennedy in Dallas, minus the Lincoln convertible.

Now, much like JFK's motorcade, the herd didn't stop moving after the lead bull went down, and it wasn't long before the group walked across Cole's field of view, and this is where things start to go awry. The only explanation I can think of is either Cole was aiming for the head, or just had bad aim, but whatever the case, he fired, and instead of activating the Presidential Line of Succession, he shot this caribou directly in the shovel. The herd, sensing something wasn't right in Dealey Plaza, began to move a little quicker, and by the time Cole got reloaded, the herd had moved to where he couldn't shoot without risking hitting TSgt Honeysett, so he had to let it go.

TSgt Honeysett picked up where Cole left off, hitting the one Cole shot, but not dropping it. At the same time, Luke took down the third bull of the group, and began to unload his gun.

By this point, that second bull had began to realize that something was seriously wrong, and took off running. Meanwhile, TSgt Honeysett had developed full-on Buck Fever. He stood up and began shouting at Luke, "Shoot that [redacted] thing!" while taking potshots at it himself. Meanwhile, Luke, who developed a case of Buck Fever of his own, was trying to get his gun reloaded, and ended up ejecting several live shells out of his rifle before he finally got it together. He fired at the fleeing caribou and managed to down it, but it wasn't yet dead. TSgt Honeysett had ran out of ammunition, but he ran over to where it lay, abandoned by the rest of the herd, and finished it off with his 9MM.

I had heard the shots and the shouting, and had debated crossing over the hill to investigate, but I didn't want to risk losing my spot to one of the road hunters, and ended up staying put. About an hour later, TSgt Honeysett came up over the hill, dressed in normal clothes, to check on me.

"See anything yet?" he asked me?

"Not a thing, sir," I replied.

"Well, wanna come try my side of the hill?"

"Sure, might as well." I picked up my pack and followed him back over the Knoll.

Now, I had to pass through the Camp Flat to get to his side of the hill, and as we passed through, I saw two caribou, hanging up on this rack we built out of dead timber, waiting to get gutted and carved up into chunks small enough to be able to pack back to the trucks, and Preston was just hanging up his at that very moment. Cole was observing where he drilled the bull TSgt Honeysett claimed, in the shovel.

That scene wouldn't have been a lot cooler if those were the last bulls we saw on the whole trip. We didn't see a thing come near the Knoll after that. So many tags were filled during the opener, Fish & Game shut the season down after the second day, and Cole and I went back to town empty handed (though the others did share a little meat with the two of us, which was cool).

Later, when TSgt Honeysett had his bull mounted, he had Cole sign it.

He used the hole he put through the shovel as the "o" in his name.

I went on several other hunting trips up there, but that's the one that stuck with me the most, and was the most successful group hunt I've ever been on. Now, I'm medically retired from the military, and really looking forward to returning to Fortymile and trying my hand again.

And I'm eligible for subsistence hunts this time.

TRAPPING TALES BY BY WARREN VANDERBURG

First published in Confessions of a Poacher
Warren Vanderburg (1906-1996)

CLARENCE GETS AN EYEFUL

The winter of 1927-1928 Clarence and I were trapping the main river [Siuslaw, in Oregon] and batched in the old schoolhouse on Karnowsky Creek; it was a rough job, not used for close to ten years. It was a box type, had a partition down the middle, as high as the plates—school on one side of the divider and woodshed on the other.

We had a lot of roast ducks that winter; at that time there were at least a hundred ducks to where there are one or two now. We were trapping, so didn't have time to really hunt, but since we were trapping the river and each had a rowboat, we could pot a roaster full about every time we needed them, which was often. Most of the birds we got were widgeons, sprigs (pintail), or mallards, and nearly all were hog fat.

Uncle Arnold had two good-sized dogs, friendly mutts, and they got in the habit of coming down to the schoolhouse and spending the night in the woodshed. They also liked the flavor of roast duck, and would chomp up the bones as fast as we got through with them; they were our garbage disposal unit. We nearly always had roast duck for supper; when we got done with the bones, we just tossed them over the partition from our table, and the bones began to crack.

We tried to get on the river as soon as we could see, and usually got back close to an hour before dark. The first one back in the evening would build a fire and start supper. In the morning we took turns about getting breakfast; one would cook for a week, then the other for a week —of course, we took a lunch for our noon meal, often a roast duck, and maybe some buck jerky, but our mainstay was a trapper's sandwich. What? You never heard of one? O.K....we nearly always had flapjacks (you may call them hotcakes, or pancakes—they are all the same) home-made; and smoked bacon, and eggs.

We knew about how many flapjacks we would eat so cooked two extra. We used a nine-inch frying pan and made the flaps full-sized. We also cut extra bacon, thick sliced, which we cooked over medium heat, fried till nearly all the grease was cooked out, but the bacon was not overcooked and brittle. When we were through with breakfast, the two extra flapjacks were cool, but not dried out. Next, instead of spreading butter on them, we used cold bacon grease, then spread on a layer of brown sugar, then covered the top with strips of bacon and rolled it up about like you would a jelly roll cake. Wrapped in paper, there was a fine tasting sandwich, and one that would stick to your ribs.

One evening I got back to camp about an hour before dark, started a fire, started supper and put our roaster full of ducks in the oven to warm up, but Clarence didn't show up by dark. I was a little worried, and stuck my head out the door every few minutes to see if he was coming. About the time it got real dark I smelled a civet cat; the wind was blowing up the canyon, but I was sure it wasn't Clarence I smelled. Just figured the civet had been disturbed by a bobcat, and had decided to teach Bobby a lesson.

Another half an hour went past, then I heard someone walking in the woodshed, and Clarence came in; also, he *was* the civet cat, and he must have been at least a mile from camp when I first got a whiff of him.

He also had a tale to tell—he was looking at some traps on Wendson Creek, above Cushman, and had a civet in a trap. He dispatched it and started to skin the critter—not a hard job, except for one thing. In skinning around the scent sac, at the root of the tail, you need a very sharp knife, and you don't want to make a mis-lick and cut into the scent gland.

It was late, the weather was about ready to spill some rain, and Clarence was in a rush. He skinned the back legs; with a heavy cord he put a loop on one back leg, tossed the loose end over a tree limb that was the right height, then put a couple of half hitches on the other leg; he then skinned the legs out the rest of the way and started to cut around the scent bag.

The light was poor and his eyes were close to where he was working; also, the civet's bushy tail was up in the way, so he took hold of the tail and pulled it down out of the way. Guess he pulled a little too hard, and the dead civet gave him a charge, right in the eyes. It blinded him, but he was only a few yards off the creek—he could hear that, so got down on his hands and knees and felt his way to the water. He washed his eyes for half an hour before he could see to walk, then had to row about two miles and walk another mile to camp.

I doubt if he ever smelled that rank again as long as he lived.

Bowing to the Creek

Warren Vanderburg

I remember a pleasant few minutes watching my cousin, John Karnowsky, look at a trap on Sutton Creek, back in the thirties. The creek was about sixty or seventy feet wide. In one place a big tree had fallen across, one end on each bank, and with some moss on the opposite end.

The only way to tell if the trap was O.K. or uncovered, or weather-sprung, was to walk across the log for a close look. The tree sagged a bit in the middle, and would sway back and forth while a person walked across. This time John was in a little too much of a rush, and started too fast; the log began to sway and bounce up and down. He made it to the trap, looked at it, almost lost his balance (he would have fallen into six or eight feet of cold water). He tried to turn around on the log to come back, his arms going like windmills.

He got turned halfway around, bowed to the creek, turned around again so he was facing upstream, made an elaborate bow in that direction, and managed to turn back facing me. Then, feeling himself about to fall, he let one foot slide off each side of the log, landed on his rump and hitched his way back to the trail on his hands and rump.

Of course, I was laughing so hard I couldn't have fished him out if he had landed head first in the creek.

The Swimming Trapper
Warren Vanderburg

My trapping partner, Clarence Hubbard, once caught a mouse in one end of a No. 2 Victor [trap], and a weasel in the other end at the same time. Apparently the weasel was chasing the mouse, and was only a few inches behind, when they got to the trap. The mouse jumped over the pan and landed straddle of the jaws, just as the weasel's front feet hit the pan and sprung the trap. Both were caught around the middle, with the weasel's nose only about an inch from the end of the mouse's tail.

When we trapped in the sand-hills in 1926-27, Clarence had one line north of Sutton Creek [central Oregon coast], where there are several small lakes of only a few acres each. In the summer and fall when the water is low, a person can walk all around them with no problem, but after a few good rain storms in the winter, the lakes will rise eight or ten feet, to the brush line. It is hard for anything bigger than a rabbit to crawl through the brush along the shore.

At one of these small lakes, open sand came down to the water line on one side; on the other side a big tree had fallen in the lake at one time, and the top reached almost to the center of the lake, while the roots were still anchored in the dirt on the opposite shore. The top of the tree had a little moss on it, and stayed above water all year around; it also had a game trail through the moss—a good set for a wandering mink.

When Clarence set a trap in the trail, the water was low and he had no problem walking around the lakeshore to check the trap. After a few heavy rains the only way he could circle the lake was to fight his way for two hundred yards through the thick brush.

If that had been on my trap-line, I would have pulled the trap, but Clarence had another idea. When he came down the sand dunes to the lakeshore, rain or shine, frost or snow, he would peel off his clothes and swim about fifty yards out to the trap, check for fur, then swim back to his clothes. Made me shiver to think about it.

When fifteen or seventeen years old, he shot ducks in one of the sloughs around here. If the ducks were too far from shore to reach with a pole, he would swim out and retrieve them—just like a good bird dog.

What may have started him doing that was a mishap he had earlier. One day he was across the river and got two or three ducks in a wide spot in a slough on the old Gene McCornack place. The ducks were about fifty yards from shore. There were some small logs and a few old boards around that had floated in during a freshet, so Clarence found a couple of short logs, about six or eight feet long.

He shoved them out in the water, leaving one end on the shore, then put three or four short boards across them for a platform to sit on, pushed the logs overboard, took a pole he had found on shore to push his raft, and went after his ducks.

It worked fine till he got out to the birds—then, since the logs were only held together by the lumber lying on them, they decided to part company. One log rolled one way, one the other way, and the platform went in the near-ice water, along with Clarence. He had to round up his ducks and swim ashore with his clothes on, then walk about 2½ miles home, soaked to the top of his head, to find dry clothes. I think that cured him of going swimming with his clothes on.

No Romantic Thoughts

Warren Vanderburg

In all the years I roamed around in the wet brush or on the water I never fell overboard. That is, not completely, but I did manage to get wet a couple of times. One cold, miserable day in the middle of the winter, when the water was almost as cold as ice, I had a little experience on Tahkenitch Lake that I never forgot. That was near the mouth of Five Mile Creek; I had a trap on the bank back of the roots of a big tree that had fallen out in the lake in some forgotten time. The roots had peeled off at the edge of the lake, and had a good clump of brush growing on them.

When I set the trap (an otter set) the lake was low and I could land my boat against the log, tie it up to a limb, then walk up to—and through—the roots and jump off on solid ground. Of course, I always wore hip boots when running traps on the lake or river in case I had to do any wading.

We had had several days of heavy rain, and the lake had raised four or five feet. When I got to the back edge of the roots the water looked too deep to jump in, even though my boots were thirty-six inches high.

A short log, about a foot and a half through, had floated in behind the stump. One end was on the bottom of the lake but the other end was out of water. I thought I could jump over to the high end of the log, then hop onto solid ground.

It didn't work. When my boots landed on the log the high end slowly began to sink, and by the time it touched bottom the ice-cold water was pouring into both boots. I couldn't jump to shore, and as I had my back to the brush on the roots behind me, I just reached back and hoped to get hold of something that wouldn't break. I was lucky. I caught a long, limber limb that bent when I pulled on it, but the log I was on slowly came to the top. When I tried to turn around and jump back toward where my boat was, the darned log just slowly sank and I shipped some more water.

The next time I pulled myself up to the top of the lake I took a chance, let go of the limb, turned and jumped for the roots. Made it, and sloshed my way out to where the boat was tied.

Since it would be hard to pull off my boots when they were over half full of water I had a bright idea—I sat down on the log and stuck one foot up in the air so the water would run back in my boot and drain out the top. The idea was fine, till I tried it. It was a nasty day, and I don't remember having any romantic notions, but if I did, they didn't last long. Instead of that cold water running out my boot top, about two gallons of it galloped up the inside of my pant leg, then joyously romped over and ran down into my other boot. Well, you can't win them all.

Outhouse Deluxe!

Warren Vanderburg

When Clarence and I trapped the sand-hills [central Oregon coast] in 1926-27, we used a fleshing knife that I had made from a fourteen-inch wood rasp when I first began trapping, about 1918. I used the same tool for fleshing all the pelts, except beaver, as long as I trapped, and I still have it.

When Clarence and I made our fur stretchers we also made three fleshing poles, one for small or medium mink, one for large and extra-large mink and one for 'coon and bobcats. I still have the small mink pole, and used it as long as I trapped. Still have it, in good condition, about sixty-eight years later.

The winter Clarence and I batched in the old Jim Bob Nelson Cabin on Sutton Creek we had a problem. We needed a powder room, or a backhouse—and didn't have time to build one. We looked around for a substitute, and we found a doozy. A bit swell-butt cedar tree had been sawed off about five or six feet above ground—sawed high to get above the swell.

Like a lot of cedar, it had several roots that ran out almost horizontal to the ground. The tree had been hollow clear to the ground and the hole in it was about three feet across. Perfect. Most of the time, we could gallop up onto the stump and perch there as long as we cared to. Only two drawbacks—when it rained we needed an umbrella, and our perch was in the front yard, only about thirty feet from the front door.

Oh well, it really didn't matter. We seldom had company.

Bear Tracks in the Sand

Warren Vanderburg

In the fall of 1926 my hunting and trapping partner, Clarence Hubbard, and I moved into a deserted cabin on Sutton Creek, a couple of hundred yards downstream from the present Highway 101. At that time, some of the road right-of-way work had been done as far as Sutton Creek, and the grade had a layer of clay on top of the sand base, to keep the gravel from sinking when they got around to finishing the job.

It could be driven before the fall rains started. After that you walked. Once the clay got soaked up, no car could get over it. Clarence and I intended to trap the sandhills, also Sutton Creek and Mercer Lake.

In those days Clarence went barefoot nearly all year around, rain, hail, sleet or snow. Sand burrs or sharp rock had no effect on him. I have seen him run a foot race on crushed gravel, and it wouldn't even scratch his hide. After we got moved to out winter headquarters, we did some scouting around the sand hills for fur sign, opened up a few trails, and figured out the lay of the land. Our next door neighbor was J.C. "Jack" Herron, who had homesteaded near Mercer Lake. We had never met him, but since we had to pass within about 100 yards of his cabin every time we went to the lake, we decided to stop in and get acquainted. The day we went for a visit, Clarence was shoeless, as usual, and was packing a little Winchester Model 92, in .25-20 caliber. It was a well-balanced rifle, with a twenty-two-inch barrel and half magazine.

When we arrived at Jack's house, he was in the yard. He seemed friendly enough and we talked a bit, and told him we would be going past his place every day or two during the trapping season.

Then Jack happened to glance down and saw Clarence's bare feet. He started to swear, and could out-swear most mule skinners. It almost scared us; we had never seen him before, and thought perhaps we had a madman for a neighbor.

Pretty soon he quit swearing and said, "I have been hunting for thirty years and never got a shot at a bear. A couple of days ago I was down Sutton Creek, looking for tracks, and found fresh bear tracks, or parts of bear tracks. There were enough weeds growing on the sand so I could see only parts of tracks, but I decided they looked fresh. So, I followed them for half a mile or so, then they led out on a little patch of clear white sand—and I discovered I had been trailing a human. Damn you, Shorty, I got a notion to shoot you." We had a good laugh, and that was the end of it.

Jack Finally Gets a Bear

Warren Vanderburg

Jack Herron said that he grew up on hid dad's nut farm near Salem, Oregon. When quite young he wanted to be a good enough shot to get a job with one of the big gun or ammo companies, as a trick shot, so he got him a pump .22 and a lot of ammo.

There were a few black walnut trees on the place and no sale for the nuts, so he got one of his dad's big nut-hauling wagons with a tight box, packed it completely full of black walnuts, then parked it by the barn. Before spring he had tossed up and broken every nut in the wagon.

He never followed up on the shooting job, but later tried his luck as a prize fighter—welterweight, I think. He wasn't very big but had long arms and was very broad-shouldered. He also did a lot of trapshooting and knew about all the big-shot sporting men around the state.

When he moved down to the sandhills he brought two shotguns: a trap-grade Remington pump, and a side-by-side double-barrel (though he used it for all his singles shooting—that is, he used just one barrel). While the barrel he didn't use was almost new, the other barrel was shot so much there was a hole worn through it just ahead of the chamber.

Since he couldn't find another gun that fit like his old pet, he got a piece of green cowhide, cut a strip about four inches wide and long enough to just reach around both barrels, then laced the patch on as tight as possible with a lacing cut from wet cow hide. He then set up the weapon in a dry, warm place for a few months till the cowhide patch dried out and shrunk so tight it was almost part of the barrels. Then he started shooting it again with no more problems.

The hunting rifle Jack brought down to the coast was a Model 99, .300 Savage—the first .300 I had ever seen. When Jack moved out to the coast he had an idea. He wanted to buy some lake frontage on Mercer Lake and start a resort. The problem was that he was flat broke, but somehow he managed to buy, I believe it was a square forty acres at the west end of the lake, and he got it on time, and hoped he could make the payments.

When I met him, he had put up a couple of small rustic cabins and had two or three row-boats. Two or three years later I worked for him, putting up another cabin or two, but mostly landscaping along the lakeshore. That fall, Jack finally got his bear, the first he had ever shot, and I believe, the last. One morning, while working on the lakeshore, we saw a black bear walking on a white log, in shallow water, on the end of the Dowell Peninsula. It stuck out about half-way across the lake about half a mile from us. Jack forgot about work. His .300 Savage was leaning against a bush near us—he went for that while I headed for a boat. As we figured it, I would put him ashore near where the peninsula left the hill; then I would take the boat out to where we had seen the bear. I would land and see if I could scare bruin back toward the hill. If so, he would be in sight of Jack when he crossed the horse trail, and not over fifty yards from his gun muzzle.

So much for trying to guess what a bear will do. When we got about halfway across the lake, with me rowing—my back to the bow of the boat, Jack in the stern—he suddenly said, "What's that black spot in the lake?" I twisted my neck around to look, said, "Bear," then dug one oar in the lake and took an extra-long stroke with the other one. We spun halfway around and were headed towards the bear, 200 or 300 yards off, and making good time toward the far shore.

Then more problems arose; on the far side of the bruin, and bearing down fast, was another boat. It was one of Jack's. That morning Charley Palmer had driven in to the lake. He wanted to borrow a boat to go fishing, but he also had his rifle along (a nice balanced little .30-30 Winchester with a twenty-four-inch round barrel and half-magazine).

Charley was closer than we were, but he hadn't the experience with oars that I had. Jack started to swear, then said, "Slim, old Charley has shot a lot of bear and I have never shot even one. If you let him beat us to that b'ar, I'm going to shoot you."

I was already putting a good bend in the oars, but now I put more. But, I was afraid if I put too much power on them, one would break. They were cedar oars, handmade, light and easy to handle but cedar is pretty brittle, and if I broke one, we were out of the race. Well, we beat Charley by about fifty yards, and Jack got his bear, his first and the only one I ever saw swimming. I have a picture around that I took of Jack and his bear, after we hung him up in a tree to butcher.

The Mighty Black Bear Hunters

Warren Vanderburg

About as stupid a thing as I ever did was go on a camping trip to hunt deer and then shoot two bear in two days. Clarence Hubbard and I intended to go camping and try for a fat buck. After all the trouble we had, mostly caused by me, it is a wonder he didn't shoot me—or at least quit speaking. The fact that he is still one of my very best friends, over forty years later, is proof that he is a forgiving sort—or very short of memory.

Clarence had a horse we could use, so we put a pack on him, and started out one fall morning, walking and leading the old plow horse. We made about fifteen miles and camped the first night in some spruce timber, just up the hill from the Sea Lion Caves, below the old wagon road—about where Highway 101 is now.

After making camp we walked up to Cape Creek, and spent the evening with friends [at the lighthouse]. Next morning we went on up the coast to Big Creek, then turned up the creek. We had never been there before, but had directions on where to turn off on the old Jack Bunch Trail. After passing Jack's homestead, and the one of Ben Bunch, it was only a short distance to the forest trail, then a left turn, and not over half a mile to the Three Buttes Cabin, a three-sided, split shake affair, put up for the occasional use of the Forest Service trail crew, and a place to store tools and a telephone.

The trail was pretty well grown up—or else we got on the wrong one. But finally we reached the forest trail, about a mile on the wrong side of the cabin.

Then the horse got loose and started toward Saddle Mountain, about six or seven miles away; but by cutting across bends of the trail, Clarence outran him and finally recovered both horse and pack. By the time we got back to the Three Buttes, and made camp, it was about dark. Soon after dark we could hear deer walking all around us. We had only a little two-cell flashlight, but one big buck walked past camp so close we could see his outline. When we turned the light on the face of the butte in front of the cabin, the eyes looked like stars.

Being young and innocent, at that time we didn't know a thing about night hunting, so all we did was look. Right behind the cabin was a small flat, covered with short salal brush and fern; after we went to bed, a herd of deer moved up to within thirty or forty yards, and snorted and stomped so we couldn't sleep.

Clarence finally got up and chased them away. When he ran around the corner of the shack with his shirt tail flapping in the breeze, the deer all fled in horror; but in half an hour were back, probably wanting another look at the strange, hairless creature that had moved into their territory.

Next morning we had breakfast before daylight. Clarence decided to hunt over toward Saddle, while I went the other way, toward Herman Peak. It was pretty dark when we left camp, but we didn't expect to see anything till we got away from camp a quarter mile or so.

The first bear I got that trip, I shot from the horse trail, less than half a mile from our camp. I got almost to where Bunch's trail branched off, when on a little bench below the trail I saw a big black blob on a big white log. So, like an idiot, I forgot all about bucks.

It was still too dark to see my sights good. The bear was on the east side of the trail, toward the strongest light, and on black hide or dark brush the sights faded out completely. But I could see them against the white log, so I took a bead under the bear, on the log, then pulled up till the bead should have been right back of the shoulder, and touched off a shot.

Bruin simply flattened out on the log and lay there. Not knowing where he was hit, I tried another shot, at the neck that time. He still stayed on top of the log, so after watching him for about five minutes I went down for a close look.

The first shot had broken his back just behind his shoulders. The second had broken his neck—and then the fun began. I rolled him off onto the ground and field dressed him. Wondering if I could drag him the 125 yards to the trail, I stepped straddle of his carcass, locked my fingers together under his middle, and tried to lift him. All I did was make a slight hump in his middle—couldn't even get one end off the ground let alone two.

Finally, I went back to camp to wait for Clarence, but he had heard me shoot, and thinking I had probably got a buck, he had beat me to camp. So we saddled up the horse and went after the bear. We had a good thirty-five-foot, half-inch rope, and by slipping a noose over the bear's lower jaw, then throwing a half hitch over his nose and lower jaw to keep his mouth shut we managed, in two hours of the hardest work we ever did, to skid him, a few inches at a time, up to the trail where, hopefully, we thought the horse could take over.

First we got the bruin pointed toward camp, then rolled him belly down. The horse took a dim view of the proceedings. He was rolling his eyes and snorting, but we managed to back him up to about twenty-five feet of the bear. Clarence got in the saddle, tied the free end of the rope to the saddle-horn—and we were off!

The old plug took the slack out of the rope, leaned into it, then glanced back to see what he was pulling on. Well, when he saw that big bear coming after him, only thirty feet behind, he shifted into overdrive and headed for camp on the run, and almost sawed Clarence's leg off with the rope.

I couldn't keep up but Clarence got him stopped as they reached camp. The day was shot, so far as deer hunting was concerned, as we were busy all day skinning out the bear, cutting up meat and nailing the hide to the cabin wall.

Since it takes a lot more work to take care of a big bear than it does to handle two or three deer, I ruined our hunt before it got started. Well, I was a lot younger [age 16-17] then than I am now.

It was the biggest bear I ever killed, or ever saw killed, but not the fattest, though I did get five gallons of good white bear grease out of the fat. We used the bear grease instead of lard or shortening, and it was preferred by most cooks for making pastry. We smoked the lean meat. Bear jerky doesn't dry out as hard as deer meat. I'm sure there would have been twenty or twenty-five gallons of lard if he had been fat. In later years I have seen people gloat over grizzly hides that were far smaller than what we peeled off that black.

The next morning Clarence again started out on the Saddle Mountain trail, and I decided to go to the top of the butte in front of camp, since I had never seen what was on the other side. The west side was almost a rock cliff, and at the base of it there was what looked to be a fairly open bench. But later we found out the brush was over head-high on it. From the top, I could see several logs, that looked to be on the ground—and on one of them stood a big black bear.

Since at best bear meat is a poor substitute for buck meat, I should have walked off and left him, but no, I had to have me another blackie. So I sat on the top of the butte, took a solid rest across my knees, and dropped a .30-30 bullet on his back—I was shooting down at about a forty-five degree angle. Bruin went over the side and out of sight, then pulled himself back on the log and I got one more shot at his rump as he dove off the end of it again, and then he was gone.

The first bullet hit a couple of inches to one side of the backbone, went through the lung and exited between the front legs. The second hit him in the rear as he jumped off the log, and went most of the way through him endways. He was one tough bruin.

When I got down to the bench, the brush was so tall, and thick, that I couldn't even find the log he had been on. So back to camp for Clarence—and again he had heard me shoot and returned to camp. This time I stayed on top and he went down in the brush. When he lost his way, he would climb up on a down tree till I was in sight, and I could motion him in the direction of the big log the bear had been on.

Once Clarence found the log, I went down; bruin had left about the best blood trail I have ever seen, and he must have been full of it. After jumping off the log, he was in a bear trail, with the brush lapped together above his back, so we had to crawl.

There was a stripe of blood in the middle of the trail, and the brush overhead was sprayed with it. We expected to find him dead any minute, but must have gone 300 yards; came out of the thick brush and into a little open, with only short salal brush and fern.

We found where he had laid down by a log, then got up and moved, but had quit bleeding. Being sure he had bled dry and would be within a few yards, we decided to separate and start circling as there were no tracks, the ground being too dry and hard.

I had gone only about twenty feet when I happened to glance at Clarence, just in time to see him leave the earth, in what must have been the world record for the standing broad jump. The bear was dead, but Clarence had stepped right between his hind feet before he saw him, and was more than a little bit startled.

To make a long story short, we didn't get any venison, but did spend the rest of our time getting a lot of third-class bear meat packed twenty miles home. When we packed up, we folded one of the bear hides and put it on the saddle. Next thing we saw was the horse coming back to earth, and the hide about three feet above the ground. By the time we got home we had walked so much we both had the squeak heel so we could hardly hobble for two weeks.

Apparently I learned slow; I had killed two bear before this trip, and should have known they cause too much work for the good you get out of it. After that I passed up all of them except an occasional fat one in the late fall, for the grease, or a small one to smoke for bacon. I knew people who hunted the same country I did, all their lives, and never even saw a bear. Maybe I just smelled right, but it seemed like every time I got out in bear country, I rubbed noses with one. I have killed between fifteen and twenty, and passed up twenty-five or thirty.

FLOUNDERING BY HARRY STEWART

A nd when the flounderer shone his light into the crab trap--well, first you need to know about floundering. And crab traps.

So, a flounder is a very tasty fish with an odd lifestyle. Flounders swim upright like normal fish while they're young. As a flounder grows up, one eye migrates across the top of its head to join the other eye on the same side of its body. After that, it lies flat on the bottom of the sea, hiding in the sand, with only its two eyes sticking out. If a tiny prey fish swims into range, it can pop up and nab it, and then flatten back out in the sand. If a big predator fish comes along, all it sees is two little spots and some more sandy bottom. Some people call this kind of fish a "sole," but on the Alabama coast, it's a flounder.

You can't easily catch a flounder with a hook. They don't swim around looking for tidbits. You would have to know where the flounder was, and drag the bait around just overhead until the flounder bites. But Mobile Bay is murky, and the flounder could be anywhere on the bottom, and trying to find one with a baited hook is just a waste of time.

So how do you catch a flounder? Wait for low tide. Mobile Bay is shallow, and its bottom is flat as a skillet. In most places, even at high tide, you can walk out a quarter mile from shore before the water is over your head. At the lowest tides, the water is ankle-deep, or maybe a little higher, up to fifty or a hundred yards offshore. And you can see pretty well through ankle-deep water.

The lowest tides happen around the night of the full moon. A day or two before that, you start watching for an afternoon squall. That will stir up the bottom and move everything around, and then kill the wind so that everything settles down again. In the evening, the daytime sea breeze will shift to a land breeze. Close inshore, the land breeze is blocked by the trees above the beach, so the water's surface is mostly flat with little ripples. With no wave action, a lot of the murk settles to the bottom, clearing up the water. On a calm night, with a low tide and a bright light, it's pretty easy to see the bottom, and the critters that live there.

So, if you have a taste for flounder, you wait for a night like that, put on some old sneakers so the barnacles don't cut up your feet, and go out wading with a bright light and a gig. A gig is a spear for fish. It can be as complicated as Poseidon's three-pronged trident, or as simple as a big nail on the end of an old broomstick. The bright lights used to be adapted from a Coleman lantern, with the mantles out in the open and a big reflector behind them, but now it's more common to use propane or electricity.

Then you wade out into the ankle-deep water, with your light in one hand and your gig in the other. Walk slowly and softly, because the flounders can sense vibrations through the sand, and they will zip away if they feel you coming. Oddly, they don't care about lights, so you shine your light out in front of you, scan it side to side, and look for a flat spot like a dinner plate among the little sand rilles on the bottom. If that flat spot has two black eyes, try to hit it dead center with the gig. This takes practice, because the water refracts the light and fools your eye. You'll hit high or low until you get used to it.

Usually, the flat spot you see is nothing. Sometimes it's a fluke of the sand and the waves. Sometimes it's a spot where a flounder used to be. But maybe once out of a hundred tries, the flat spot you stuck your gig into starts flapping like mad, and that's a flounder. Hold the gig down to the sand with one hand, reach around with the other, and grab the gig point underneath the flounder to keep it from sliding off. Then pick up the gig and flounder together, open up your creel, and drop it in. Clean them when you get home, pop them in the icebox, and serve them up for dinner the next day.

Flounders are tasty, but crabs are tasty too, and they're easier to catch. In Mobile Bay, these are blue crabs the size of a man's hand, not the monsters that come from Alaska. You can catch crabs with a net, and you can pick them up off the bottom while you're looking for flounder, but the easiest way by far is to use a crab trap.

A crab trap is a chicken-wire cube about two feet on a side. Inside, it has some baffles and a bait well, all made of chicken wire, too. It works on the same principle as a Maine lobster pot. There are two or three funnel-shaped entrances cut through the outside and the baffles, leading to the bait in the middle. The funnels are smooth on the wide side and have lots of pointy chicken-wire stubs on the narrow side. The crab crawls in through the funnels the easy way, eats its fill of the bait, and then isn't smart enough to find its way back out.

If you want a meal of tasty crab claws, you fill the bait well with whatever cheap meat you have handy, attach the trap by a line to a pier or a buoy, then drop it into the water so the bait well winds up on the bottom. Wait a couple of days, then haul up the trap and see what you got. If you're too impatient, you get nothing; if you wait too long, the crabs start eating each other. One corner of the trap opens up, so you shake all the crabs into that corner and then reach in and grab them one by one. Cowards use tongs, but real men just reach in and grab a crab between the flippers and the shell, where its claws can't quite get back far enough to nip you.

To clean a crab, first you break off both the claws and drop them in a pail of fresh water. Then you jam one point of the shell into any handy piece of wood, take the other point in one hand and the legs on that side in the other, and pull hard to separate the top shell from the body. Break the rest of the legs and the flippers off the body, clean the innards out, and drop it in the pail with the claws. The rest is trash, or chum. Rush that pail full of bodies and claws into the kitchen, fill a big pot with clean water, and start boiling them. If you're lucky enough to find a soft-shelled crab, just after it molted--but that's another story.

There are all kinds of recipes for crab boil, but if you just buy a jar of Zatarain's and follow the instructions, you won't go too far wrong.

They're cooked when the blue and green on the claws turn to scarlet and pink. Then you have to get the meat out of the shells. It's traditional to serve crab claws whole, so the guests get the fun of pulling the big claw muscle out of its shell. But cracking the bodies apart and picking the meat out of all the little crevices is tedious. Often, you just stick the bodies in the icebox after boiling them, and pull them out when you've got some free time. Picking crab is a good after-supper pastime, as you watch the sun sink into the bay and the kids play on the beach.

One day, when I was about six, my teenage cousins took their .22 rifles and went plinking out back by the swamp. We call it a "wetland" now--sounds classier--and you can't just casually shoot back there any more, because there are lots more people around, and you have to be careful about your backstops. But in those days, there was nothing wrong with teenagers hunting varmints way out back.

They came back all excited, carrying a long-eared rabbit they got with a lucky shot. They were getting ready to skin it and clean it when their father stepped in. He checked the rabbit for parasites, and found that it was full of worms. Well, you can't eat wormy meat, so there went the idea of rabbit stew. And what were they going to do with the dead rabbit?

Dad pointed out that the crab trap was almost out of bait. Crabs will eat anything, anything at all, and turn it into delicious crabmeat. So my two cousins walked out the pier, hauled up the trap, turned it over, stuffed the rabbit into the bait well ears first, and dropped it back in the water. Half an hour later, a squall hit, and in the thunder and lightning we forgot about the crab trap.

Later that night, after dinner, we were all out on the screen porch, enjoying a warm summer evening. Mom and Dad were picking crabs, and my brothers and I were playing Monopoly because the squall had killed the breeze and the bugs were too thick to go outside. Once it got too dark to see the board, Dad started telling stories about the Bay when he was a kid. And then we saw a flounderer down the beach with his light, working his way toward us.

Most people go out floundering for fun on a nice evening, and quit when they've found enough for tomorrow's dinner. But some folks earn a bit of extra cash selling flounders to restaurants. They're out every night around the full moon, moving up and down the beaches, sometimes poling a little flat-bottomed boat with a bow-mounted light rather than wading. Dad preferred to wait for the full moon and the lowest tide, but the professionals took every chance they could get. And this was the night before the full moon, when the low tide came earlier in the evening.

Dad kept telling stories in a low voice as the flounderer made his way up the beach. The usual murmured debate started as he came up to our pier. Would he stick to shallow water and go under, or would he go around, out into water that might be too deep to see a flounder? Walkers usually went under, but he was in a small boat, poling it forward. Boats usually went around, and poles might not fit under the pier. But he headed straight for the pier, as if he were planning to go under.

He didn't, though. As he got up to the pier, he let out a yell, and his light jumped sideways. He turned it back toward the pier and yelled again, and his light jumped again. He turned the light very slowly toward the pier, one last time. When the light reached the space underneath the pier, he shouted something I didn't quite catch, about something shining. We heard a kerplunk far offshore, like a fish jumping, but bigger. Then he turned off his light, turned his boat around, and poled quickly back down the beach. Dad was laughing so hard he nearly fell out of his chair, but quietly, because sound carries over water. We all watched the flounderer move through the moonlit glints off the water, down the beach, around the point, and out of sight.

Once he was gone, Dad got a floundering light out of the shed, lit it, and invited us all to come see what the flounderer saw. We waded out beside the pier until we got to the spot where the flounderer had started to cross under. Dad suddenly swung the light around, shining under the pier. And we all saw it at once.

Under the pier, mostly out of the water at low tide, was the crab trap. Only its bait well was submerged. And in the bait well was the rabbit, feet down on the ocean floor, with its long ears moving gently in the ripples on the water. The chicken wire of the crab trap was almost invisible in the Coleman light, and the crabs hadn't really started in on the rabbit's carcass. It looked for all the world like a real live water-breathing rabbit, sitting calmly on the sandy bottom. We all had a good laugh at the flounderer's expense. But it took years before I figured out just why Dad had been laughing so hard earlier.

The next day, my brothers and I were playing on the beach, and I found a glass canning jar that had drifted in on the tide. Nothing unusual about that; the tide brought us something new every day. The only thing at all unusual was that the jar hadn't been in the water long. No barnacles, no slime, and the glass was still clear instead of sand-scratched and purplish. It was half-full of some nasty-smelling liquid, so I dumped it out, rinsed it out with bay water, and brought it in to Grandma, who would need every canning jar she could find when it came time to make her famous fig preserves. She thanked me and washed it properly and set it up on the shelf with the rest, and I very nearly forgot about it.

It wasn't until fifteen years later, when I was telling some college friends the story of the rabbit in the crab trap, that I remembered the kerplunk, and the canning jar, and Dad's laughter, and the flounderer's yells--and the penny finally dropped. What the flounderer had actually shouted, after the third time his light showed him a water-breathing rabbit, and just before he pitched his Mason jar into the bay, was, "Darnit, I knew there was something wrong with that 'shine!"

12

REAL MEAT AND THE CITY GIRL BY GRETCHEN SCHLEYER

At the tender age of eighteen, I married a man who was a hunter. He and his brothers hunted regularly in the seasons assigned to squirrels, rabbits, deer and turkey; and during the warmer season, gigged frogs and fished in the rivers. When the weather turned cool and hunting season opened, out came the rifle or shotgun.

Hunting for food in the woods was a foreign notion to me, having grown up in the city. I only walked in the woods with my aunt as we identified the birds, and listened to their calls. As for squirrels, we fed them peanuts at the back door of her house, and watched them scampering among the trees. Meat was purchased in a meat market, not hunted in the woods.

The leaves were in full color on the crisp fall day when we newlyweds went for a walk in the Pennsylvania woods, not far from his mother's home. The woods were beautiful, and full of birds and squirrels, but there was danger. The flat rocky outcroppings were favorite hiding places for the well camouflaged poisonous copperhead snakes. While I kept a wary eye open for them, my husband Jack was busy counting the plentiful population of squirrels. It was hunting season and he was ready to go. Early the next morning. Jack and his brother Glen went squirrel hunting.

The brothers returned from the hunt by late afternoon, and Jack called for me to come outside and see what they brought. My first look at what the boys had bagged during their squirrel hunt, was an eye-opener. There in their mother's back yard were more than twenty squirrels, hanging by their tails on the clothes line, like a load of laundry. My first reaction was, "Oh, those poor dead squirrels!" The brothers laughed.

Their mother came out ooing and ahhing, and casually asked if they wanted squirrel for dinner. All agreed. Taking the carcasses from the line, the boys headed to the basement to clean their quarry. Seeing the squirrels after the cleaning would be an even bigger eye-opener.

It wasn't long before I was called down to the basement to see how a squirrel is cleaned. I thought I'd just be shown one squirrel being cleaned, so I figured I could handle that. Well, the squirrels had all been gutted and skinned except for their heads and tails. Their furry coats hung inside out from their back paws, as the headless bodies clung with skinned paws to the basement clothes line. Every muscle and sinew was now exposed and the dark red meat shone in the light of the overhead bulb. That sight would not be forgotten.

Breathlessly, I ran upstairs to the kitchen and explained the horrible sight to my mother-in-law. She had seen it all many times, and just laughed, calling down to the boys, to bring up the meat for dinner.

You have to picture cooking on a stove that had no counter area on either side. There was only a small three-tiered rolling metal cart to hold supplies. Work space was tight. Two iron skillets sizzled with butter and fat while a pan of seasoned flour sat next to the burners. The boys brought up pans of those little four-legged bodies, now trimmed into pieces, and set them on the cart next to the stove. Their mother seasoned and floured the squirrels' arms, legs, and backs. Then, it was a matter of browning and slow cooking in the pans.

The smell of cooking squirrels soon permeated the house and the aroma was very much like chicken and beef combined. Once cooked, if I hadn't seen the little creature in the raw, I could have thought of it as a piece of chicken-the dark meat. Oh, if only...

Brown gravy topped the seared and braised squirrel, along with boiled and buttered potatoes. No amount of gravy could drown the unforgettable images of the skinned animals still hovering before me. My appetite was killed, for eating squirrel.

The brothers also hunted deer, but "Bambi" was professionally butchered and presented wrapped, as steaks, roasts and ground meat. That I could handle, and I enjoyed many a venison steak or ground meat patty, mixed with pork for added fat content.

When frog gigging was in season, my mother-in-law also fixed frog legs, and I did try them. It didn't really taste like chicken to me, but like a chicken that had waded in a muddy river. Nothing like KFC.

Jack's mother raised her own chickens, so seeing a chicken she had raised from a peep, killed, cleaned and cooked, from scratch was another unforgettable eye-opener. One evening when the moon shone full across the yard, my husband called for me to look out into the back yard. He and his brother were preparing to catch and kill two of their mom's chickens. These would be our Sunday dinner, the next day.

After running around the yard, while cunningly calling to the unsuspecting birds, the squawking chickens were captured and taken, feet first, to meet their end. The end came on the base of an old stump, at the end of an axe. Thunk!... went the axe and up sprang the headless chicken, spraying out its life's blood as it ran sightless around the yard, at least two times. Jack and his brother laughed at my shocked reaction. Their mother just shook her head at that city girl's ignorance of the real world of meat. Sunday's dinner of roasted chicken, with all the trimmings was delicious.

In the basement, the floors and counters had been scrubbed, and the boy's blood-stained shirts soaked in the laundry tub.

I decided ever after to shop for my meat at the grocery store.

From "That Reminds Me" and "Life on the Planet" by Gretchen R. Schleyer

13

HOUSTON HUNTERS BY RODNEY L. SMITH

It was a month before Christmas and our dorm's brain trust was in the lounge figuring out which local tree lot was going to donate us a tree for our festivities and general decking of the hall. Of course, the tree lots were so busy this time of year that us asking them for a tree when they were out there for the taking would have just added more stress on the lot operators, so we didn't bother them with the needless and time-consuming details of making change, carrying the tree, and tying it to the car roof. This allowed them more time to spend with their paying customers. See, we were actually looking out for their interests. We left the Optimists alone because they were doing it for charity, not profit.

As the brain trust discussed the lots' security measures, ingress and egress routes to and from the various tree lots, they failed to post a security team behind them. Our head resident's relatively young and cute wife had walked out of their apartment and into their midst. I walked over to watch the show. They were busted while pondering whether wearing their bedsheets as winter camouflage would be effective when there hadn't been a measurable snow fall in Huntsville, Texas since Sam Houston lived here in the Steamboat House. (Google it)

She chewed them up one side and down the other, informing them they would not be bringing stolen property into her dorm. "We are surrounded by the entire Sam Houston National Forest. Surely, we can find a suitable tree in 163,000 acres of forest."

There was a certain logic to what she said, but don't call me Shirley.

We got out our maps and found an area that had been clearcut and replanted a few years before and was the most likely source for an appropriately sized tree.

We set out the next day into the depths of deepest darkest East Texas, inhabited by harmless armadillos, venomous snakes of various shapes, color, and sizes, canny white-tailed deer, and the deadly Houston Hunter. The Houston Hunter is a peculiar beast that still exists to this day in isolated corners of the forest. Back in the mid-70s, their weapons of choice were either a replica M-1 carbine or a Model 94 Winchester bought from a certain military surplus store, or any sporting goods store during their hunting season sales.

Neither weapon was taken to a range before hunting season to sight it in. They must have figured that was the factory's job. They'd buy one box of ammo and drive the 80 miles from Houston to Huntsville and shoot at any movement or noise, in hopes of bagging a deer, because we all know that deer make so much noise as they move about. As a result, we had vowed never ever to go into the forest unarmed during hunting season. Out of the five of us, only the head resident's wife was not armed. It was a Thursday and early afternoon. We'd be fine. Houston Hunters generally, usually, almost always came up just on the weekends. What could go wrong?

I parked outside a timber trail and was walking in the lead. We were about 100 yards in on a forestry road when we came to the head of a short road that ended at a semi-abandoned rocking horse oil pump. The dirt sprung up at my feet followed simultaneously by a loud crack to my right. I was distracted at the time, so, my remembrance of events is unclear. This chain of events was told to me over and over and I had no cause to doubt them.

My friends said I did a quickdraw that would have made a wild west gunslinger proud. I was carrying a Smith & Wesson model 15, .38 special revolver, in a thumb snap holster and next I remember it was in my hand and pointed in the direction the shot came from.

What I saw over my sights was a "hunter" with a half smile-half smirk on his face in recoil from a scoped Winchester model 94, in a rickety metal folding chair on a platform of 2x4s and plywood about 12 feet up a pine tree. He came down out of recoil with the weapon still pointing at me and his eye looking through the scope. To discourage him from further unsportsmanlike behavior, I sent a round down his way. The realization that a bullet, a solid lead, 148 grain, Keith-style, semi-wadcutter, to be exact, was headed somewhere in his general direction caused him to lose situational awareness—like the fact that he was sitting rather precariously on a metal folding chair on a piece of plywood nailed12 feet up a tree.

He was startled by my shot and to see me standing there with my pistol pointed toward him. It would have been a long shot, but I think I could have hit him once I steadied myself. He shifted back in his chair and he and it fell ass over teakettle all the way to the ground, him landing on his shoulders and the chair landing on him. He lay there breathing heavily for a few seconds before jumping up, pulling his rifle barrel out of the mud, and running like hell, now that four pistols were pointing at him.

The head resident's wife was slow on the uptake, but she figured out finally we'd been shot at. "That guy shot at us, didn't he? Did you hit him? Did you try to?"

"Yep, he sure did and no I didn't in answer to both questions. I hope he enjoys his sore shoulder tomorrow."

A half hour later, hiking out like a herd of turtles and making lots of noise, we had a pine tree about five feet tall and a little better looking than a Charlie Brown tree. We carried the tree out past where we had been shot at before, with my buddies commenting over and over about my quick draw. When we reached the entrance road, my stomach turned upside down. Sitting behind my car was a Walker County Constable.

"Okay, everybody be cool. We didn't break any laws. Let's not spend the rest of the day with this guy. Answer his questions, but don't volunteer anything."

The constable got out as we emerged and walked up to us. "Y'all don't look like you've been hunting."

The head resident's wife lost her mind at that point and ran up to the constable. "Some asshole shot at us, and it wasn't because he mistook us for a deer!"

The constable took a step back from the snarling woman. "Calm down, ma'am, and tell me what happened."

Be cool had a different meaning to her as she told him everything, just everything, including my minor part in it.

The constable came over to me. "You want to tell me your version of events?"

I told him my version, filling in what our head resident's wife hadn't seen or already told him. I walked him down to where it happened, showed him the bullet scrape in the road, and where the shooter had been. When I showed him where the shooter had buried his muzzle in the mud he started laughing.

"Okay, that hunter probably got bored and inadvertently picked somebody to play with that could shoot back. I'm going to have you fill out field contact cards and you can go."

We filled out the cards and he helped us tie the tree to my roof. He waved and shouted "Merry Christmas!" as we drove off.

That was our first and only Christmas tree foray into the forest during hunting season. We took up a collection and bought a fake tree the next year. I fully expected that the fellow we had the altercation with might consult law enforcement, but I never heard anything back on my little shoot out.Nevertheless, I kept a watch out for any undue police presence near our dorm.

After word of my quick draw got around, thumb snap holsters became a lot more common on our trips to the forest for target practice. I was sure somebody would put a bullet crease down their leg, but nobody did.

I never told them that draw was the result of hours before a mirror practicing with an unloaded pistol.

14

JOSH BY T.M. CALDWELL

One fall in the early 80's Dad and I were hunting on our family's land in Northeast Texas. Dad and Grand Dad had hunted along the old rail bed there since probably the late 40's. The covey of quail that lived there were fairly cunning as a result. I had my Grand Dad's old Savage Stevens 20 gauge double barrel, and Dad had his Browning

We also had a secret weapon along in the form of a black and white English Setter bird dog named Josh - Knight's Josh Caldwell to the AKC.

Josh had been the runt of the litter, but he was the one that sniffed the ground all the way to my parents when they went to get him from the breeder up in Idabell. All the other puppies were more interested in getting petted. Josh hunted his way over from the kennel. He passed the interview right there.

Mom had made numerous comments about how she wasn't so sure she wanted a cold hard bird dog, but Dad liked to hunt, so she agreed to try it. I believe the puppy slept in her lap all the way home from Oklahoma. Objection squashed. He was her dog from then on.

Her dog that is, until Dad opened the door to the closet where the shotgun case and his insulated coveralls were stored. The dog could barely contain his excitement at that point..

He'd bounce around wagging furiously until everything was ready, and then drag dad to the truck. Hunting was serious business to JoshHe was good enough that out in the field, you could tell if he was pointing quail or something else by the angle of his tail. Up was junk, straight back was quail. Or flies, if he was practicing in the off season in the office of the airport where we had our family business.

Which brings us back to the old rail bed. I'm not sure how long the actual tracks have been gone, but if you know what you're looking at, you can still see where they'd been. The woods had grown in close around most of it by then, but there were a few clearings. After a couple of hours wandering around the woods, we had walked into one such about 50 feet across. Josh was in the clearing in a rather uncertain looking point.

That was odd for Josh. He was in the middle of the clearing, at a point, tail at about 45 degrees. Message unclear. Dad and I quietly walked up near him and he turned his head to look at us. That was odd too. His point usually had great form - head straight ahead. Birds that way.

Looking around was not usually part of the drill. He was quivering even.

Something weird was going on.

So dad switched to his calm, quiet Flight Instructor / Golf voice, and said "Where're the birds, Josh?"

Josh looked back at us again with an expression that I suspect was meant to convey "Are you BLIND?", then barked once.

Josh had a very deep bark for as small a dog as he was. One bark was all it took. At the "WOOF!", easily a hundred quail scattered for the tree line in all directions.

We were standing in the middle of the covey. The whole clearing was suddenly a very target rich environment.

The pre-flight brief was that Dad would take left, I would take right, and we'd make sure not to shoot the dog. To me at least, this didn't really cover the "WE ARE SURROUNDED BY BIRDS" scenario we found ourselves in. But I figured "Shoot a bird" was likely a good move.

It took a second for each of us to recover - a hundred quail taking flight all around you in the woods is a bit startling. Once we were back in the game, we each picked a target and fired. Right about about in the middle. So of course, we both shot the same bird within half a second. Two little bursts of fluff in rapid succession. One down.

We both then looked for a second shot, but found none. They'd made it to the trees by that point.

Fairly cunning, like I said.

I don't think we were quite up to the dog's standards that day. He'd sneaked his way into the middle of a clearing full of birds without spooking them. All that work, and a perfect setup.

For one bird.

But he'd done his part. I'm sure he would have done it all over again. Hunting was the thing.

Josh was a very good dog indeed.

❧ 15 ❧

THE SUICIDAL DEER BY JL CURTIS

It was a dark and... well; it was dark... The usual suspects were at our annual get together in SE Colorado that was supposed to be a hunt weekend, but somehow ended up being a lot of turning money into smoke and noise, and popping a few prairie dogs, which we'd been doing all day. Because of the distance back to town, there was the usual caravan of four to six vehicles heading back in, when a suicidal buck challenged the lead Dodge 318 to a race across the road.

Needless to say, the deer lost, but not before disabling the Dodge and staggering off into the field next to the county road. Of course, we all stopped, and the search began. One of the folks riding in the Dodge was *not* a country boy, but tagged along as the search began. The ranch owner and sheriff were notified and were on the way to our location by this time.

Oh, by the way, we were all armed with a variety of pistols (this comes into play in a bit). The deer was located, and the country boy that found it drew his pistol and poked it in the eye to make sure it was dead. Four more of us walked up, and each of us did the same thing (Country folks learn 'early' to make sure whatever they've shot is actually dead and not just knocked out. Poking anything in the eyeball will get a reaction, even if it is unconscious). The city boy looked around at us and asked, "Is this a thing or what?"

One wag might have answered with words to the effect that, "If that sumbitch so much as twitches, a bullet through the brainpan pays the insurance!" Laughter ensued, and the decision was made to drag said deer back to the road and gut it out, since it appeared most of the meat was going to be salvageable.

That damned deer gained at least 75 pounds before it ever got back to the road! Once there was a light on it, the decision was to 'harvest' it, country boys and all that, waste not want not. And harvesting the meat is actually Colorado law... game meat *must* be salvaged if at all possible. If wildlife officers are notified, they'll gut and skin it and typically donate to a family in need.

Giving the driver of the Dodge the honors, the first thing was to get the head off. The ranch owner had arrived and produced a battery powered Sawsall that made quick work of that.

The deer head was placed on the hood of the Dodge to get it out of the way, as the harvesting began. *Somebody* put an orange gimme cap on the deer's head, and somebody else put a lit cigarette in its mouth as a vehicle approached from the direction of town. Meanwhile, the deer carcass was being skinned out with another gent holding the legs of the deer apart.

The vehicle turned out to be a Sheriff's Deputy (let's call him Officer Bright and Shiny, on either his first of second solo shift with the SO), who got out and approached the mass of people and vehicles slowly, not knowing what he was encountering. He flashed his light over the deer head, went by it, then back to it, and I watched his hand go to the butt of his pistol, as the Dodge owner was simulating a sex act on the deer and extolling the virtues of opposable thumbs.

Officer Bright and Shiny shined his light over the group of folks standing around the deer and realized everyone was armed, laughing, and offering commentary, when Officer Bright and Shiny said something. That got everybody's attention, and several folks noted his stance and obvious *discomfort* at what he was seeing. A number of badges were quickly produced, and the situational dynamics calmed down immediately.

About that time, a tech employed by Parks and Wildlife showed up to collect the deer head, along with an ambulance. The owner of the Dodge was, shall we say, less than happy when he was told he had to surrender the deer head for forensic examination because of the accident. Something to the effect of, "What do you mean I have to give it up? That's the biggest damned deer I ever killed and an eight point at that with a nice spread! Why, that is something like a one forty-one fifty on the Boone and Crockett scale!"

The tech was adamant, and the female paramedic on the ambulance chimed in words to the effect, "That's not a big deer. Maybe one twenty-one thirty. Ain't that big. It might go two hundred..." A *discussion* ensued, with neither side conceding any points, and it was called a draw by cooler heads, with the ambulance departing, and the tech taking the head and disappearing in the other direction.

I was at the back of the line 'directing' traffic when Officer Bright and Shiny walked back to where I was standing. His aside to me was, "I thought y'all were drunk. Now I realize y'all are just crazy!" He shook his head, looked around and wandered off as the deer harvest was completed.

Everything was packed up, cleaned up, and the disabled Dodge 318 was towed into town by one of the group, and everyone dispersed back to their homes the next day. The Dodge was repaired, and the owner returned home with his harvested deer meat, which I'm sure he ate with a smile on his face, vengeance being best served hot with a side of potatoes and greens!

Fast forward to the current day ten years and some later, and Officer Bright and Shiny's original call to the SO dispatcher is *still* being used as a training tape for the *unusual situations* an officer might encounter while on patrol...LOL

NOTE - NAMES NOT USED TO 'PROTECT' THE IDENTITIES OF THE GUILTY or innocent depending on your point of view...

❧ 16 ❧

HUNTING HOGS BY DENTON SALLE

The boy and I picked up Frank at DFW airport, the big one in Dallas, and hauled him 3 hours southeast to a friend's family farm out in the middle of East Texas. Vaguely near Tyler, the rancher, old Les's daddy, raised mostly beef cattle and hay. And pretty granddaughters according to the boy.

Don't know why I call him the boy. He's my height although a bit rangier, got his own business that pulls in a half mill a year, and has generally turned into a decent young man. Well, except for the tendency to steal tools from his father. Gets that from his momma.

Anyway, this Frank fellow, who I was working for back then, is a Yankee from Ohio and he wanted to go hog hunting. Now, if you know anything about Texas, you know feral hogs are a bit of a problem. Kinda like the locusts in Egypt were when Moses was negotiating labor terms with the Pharaoh.

Dang things are everywhere, and they'll eat anything. They damaged crops, bothered the cattle and worse, in my other son's opinion, one tried to eat his dog. That son, the oversized one, killed his first hog when it chased one of the family standards into the back of the truck. That's standard as in full-sized poodle; good hunting dogs but sane enough to know a mama hog means it's safer in the truck.

I think he shot that hog a dozen times.

You don't mess with a man's dog.

Anyway, Frank wanted to try for a big one so he could get a mount out of it. If you're shooting one over 150 pounds —I'd personally say 100 — you might as well hope for a good set of tusks 'cause it's gonna be dang near uneatable: foul-tasting and probably wormy. The little guys, with the stripe that makes them look kinda like bacon, are best.

We chatted about it for a bit, and finally decided that Les's kin probably wouldn't scar him too much. Besides I'm sure his insurance covered therapy if they did.

So we picked him up, stuffed him in the truck, and headed down. He had a ton of luggage, including a rifle case. He had done the paperwork to hunt in Texas and dealt with the mess of bringing his AR-10 along. A 300 Win Mag. Seems like a bit much gun even for a hog, but whatever.

Heck of a lot of the locals use a knife actually. We'll get to that.

❧

LES'S DADDY HAD STARTED RENTING THE OLD TRAILER ON THE property to city fellas who wanted to hunt pigs. He was charging a couple hundred a day for food, hunting, and a place to sleep. I was surprised to find he had decided that he'd put the boy and me in the house, cause, "y'all are family at this point. Your friend mind sleeping on a couch?"

Which was kinda nice as the food would be better. Mrs. Baker was off visiting her daughters in Denton, so I suspected I was going to be cooking for him and us. Not that I minded: working a grill paid for school long ago. He'd had the paying guests fed with his ranch hands. Ranch was big enough he had four-five guys working for him. There was a bunkhouse around back and some lady came by and cooked for the hands. She just made extra when they had hunters. Wasn't great food but it was authentic Texas country. Customers loved it.

We drove around to the farmhouse, parked, and got swamped with dogs when we got out. As Mr. Baker said, you don't need to buy dogs in the country 'cause city people leave them for you. The fuzzy horde recognized the boy from previous visits and Frank and I ended up unloading as he was buried in dogs.

Well, as happens we didn't have a lot of luck the first couple of days. Now, it was summer in Texas but I don't think we ever broke 110. But Frank suffered. Kept muttering about ungodly heat. Probably didn't help that he played poker with the hands and Mr. Baker. And that always involved a fair bit of drinking.

I didn't do that after the first time. Too much alcohol and too much losing money for my taste. They emptied a 120-buck bottle of scotch in 15 minutes and took me for 150 bucks the only time I was silly enough to play. I figured, yay, I was throwing him to the sharks but better him than me.

So, I bought my way out with the hooch I brought and left. The boy —I guess I should tell you his name is Tommy—wandered off and did something. Les's daughter wasn't here this time so I didn't worry. Well, not too much. I was disappointed his baby sister wasn't around either. Man, she was a hoot.

So, four the next morning I woke the kid and Frank. As expected, the kid was grumpy. He got up though and headed out to the truck. Frank, however, looked like he was gonna die.

"I played poker until one," he said.

"How much did you lose?" I asked. Rude I know, but…

"I don't want to talk about it. I don't want to ever smell corn liquor again either."

I just handed him a black coffee and told him to gear up. While he was trying to remember what he needed, the kid came back, grabbed some coffee, and headed back out. He was going to hunt the river bottom, where we had put a blind up earlier in the season.

I fired up the truck and we drove over to the back forty. After parking the truck, we crossed the bridge over the little stream that fed the cattle pond. We walked in silence and Frank used his red-tinted flashlight. Not that we needed it with the full moon and the well-worn road. It was gonna be a glorious morning.

I worried a bit on the way as Frank seemed to be sleep-walking and when we got to where the trails to the blinds split off, he stood there as if he was asleep while standing up. He was still standing when the path took me into the trees at the end of the field. I left him there. I figured worse case a cow would wake him up. Shame I didn't have salt actually...

I reached the blind by the edge of the east-most field and climbed up. Dang, even with these new knees, ladders were hard. The blind was ten feet up and looked east at a couple of deer feeders and the edge of the large tank—you might call it a pond—that made up the eastern edge of the Baker's land. It was a good-sized blind, almost eight by five, which was one of the reasons I liked hunting it. I've been known to drag a sleeping bag and spend the night so I could hunt the morning. It wasn't the worst place for that: carpeted floor, a couple chairs, tight-fitting windows and door. I've slept rougher.

In the dark, I could hear deer moving and eating—I swear they are as loud as cows—and as the dawn broke, the larger bucks disappeared. Good sized racks, probably because they were smart enough to not stay. The does and yearlings stayed longer.

As the day opened, more things moved. Hawks flew by. Other birds called out. I heard squirrels barking. But no shots.

❧

THE PATTERN REPEATED SELF FOR THE NEXT THREE HUNTS: BEAUTIFUL summer weather, mornings in the high eighties and nineties, evening in the high nineties to low hundred as the day's heat relaxed. A lot of Texas's heat comes from sunlight and even some hundred plus days up here aren't bad if you aren't in the sun. Frank might disagree.

Days were spent fishing in the pond, napping, or drinking beer and swapping lies. But Frank was getting anxious, and so Mr. Baker called a friend who loaned us a couple of night scopes. Yeah, it's legal to hunt hogs at night. Heck, I don't think they care how you kill the pests as long as you do.

So Frank and the boy spent the day sighting in and getting ready. While they were doing that, Les's kid sister turned up with her daughter, Madison. Next thing I knew, Monica, who I had met when I taught college and she would use my office to dress for interviews, was in coveralls, a white men's shirt, and cowboy boots with her ponytail pulled through a gimme cap. Had the symbols from the Gonzales flag and the motto changed to "F- around and find out." After hugging her Daddy, I got a hug too.

Madison was in tight blue jeans and a tee shirt that read "Will barrel race for pretties." She waved to Tom from the car, but headed over to kiss her Pawpaw hello.

We all chatted for a bit and then Monica dragged me into a hayloft to look at these cedar slabs her momma put up before she died. Monica wanted a table from one and so we spent a few hours shifting them, looking for the best one in terms of grain and cracks, and sweating dang near to death.

Afterwards, she proposed a dip in the pond. Good idea. Her coveralls and shirt were soaked and I wasn't any drier. After we headed back to the house, Madison, aka Maddy, was waiting with Noah and Frank on the porch. Dang, the girl's in junior college now. Off to A&M next year.

"Why are you two all wet?" Maddy asked

"Pond's full of water," Monica said.

"You two didn't skinny dip? Oh, Lord, Momma. Don't tell me you did."

"What? And put these clothes back on? No way!" Monica looked shocked. "You know how dirty the loft in Pawpaw's hay barn is. Besides I figured riding back buck-naked with the professor would upset you."

Maddy just rolled her eyes.

"The professor?" Frank asked.

"Monica met me when I was teaching at the uni. Her family already has a cousin with my name, so they started calling me that." I answered.

"Momma, if the professor is okay with it, can we shoot his big 50?" Maddy asked, doing the anime eye thing at me.

"You've been holding out on me, old man?" Frank asked. "You have a 50 BMG here?"

"Yep, it's in the truck," I said, and then to the boy, "You know it's okay, why are y'all even asking?"

"Maddy wasn't sure that her Momma was okay with it and I got better manners than to touch your gun without asking. I raised right despite your efforts." The boy answered. Mouth on him needs washing, but he's a bit big for that.

"There are doubts about that. Yeah, it's fine. Now let Miss Monica and me at the beer. That barn is hot. When you're done shooting, there's a slab that needs to go into the truck."

"Okay, for what?"

"Gonna put legs on it and make a table for Miss Monica. We dragged it out of the loft." I grinned. "Why do you think I bring you, boy?"

"There are two actually, Tom," Monica said. "I figure the other one will pay for your Daddy's work."

"Probably mine and the freak's work..." the boy muttered. But he and Maddy ran over to the truck and started pulling stuff out. Frank looked over at us, sitting with our beers.

"The freak?" Frank asked.

"His baby brother. He's got six inches and about 50 pounds on Tom. Tom's bitter."

"Mind if I go with the kids?" Frank asked.

"Nope. More the merrier. You'll like her. East Ridge Arms. She shoots like a dream," I answered and he headed over to the truck. We watched as he wobbled a bit when Tom handed him 50 pounds of competitive grade gun. Well, not really, but it feels like it when you're carrying it.

"So they gonna night hunt, Daddy says?" Monica asked.

"Yep, we'll see if they have any better luck. There are some big fellows and Frank wants a mount," I said as I watched the three of them loading stuff into the mule. A couple of hours of quiet at least.

"Sure are. But they got big by not being stupid."

I nodded in agreement and put my feet up on the porch railing. Time for a nap.

❦

MAKE A LONG STORY SHORT, THEY DIDN'T. HEADED OUT AT 11 PM AND came back empty-handed about 3 am. I talked to Mr. Baker and as I thought, he knew someone, a cousin, who ran dogs.

Now hunting deer with dogs is illegal in Texas these days, but hogs are fine. Heck, we don't even require a license for them anymore. We just want them shot. But it always surprised me how a hog, which will go for a man or even a lone dog, will run from them in a pack. Three seems to be the magic number.

Anyway, a little after lunch—chicken-fried venison steaks with country-fried potatoes and green beans from Mr. Baker's patch—this old, once-red pickup turns up. Driver's in coveralls and a gimme cap. Three, no, four very large dogs in the back. Guy driving spits into an old coffee cup and gets out. Not a tall man, but solid. Looked hard, like he worked for a living instead of riding a desk like I do.

Mr. Baker greeted him jovially, "Hey, Easy Money, you made it."

"Yeah, business was slow so I figure chasing hogs would be more useful," the man said. "Who's interested in running with the dogs?"

Mr. Baker gestured. "The professor's boy here and one of their friends. Some of the hunters in the trailer. Maybe my granddaughter. Professor, this here is Jake and he and I go back to our high school days."

"Always surprised they let you graduate. Let's talk about it for a bit. Any of them ever killed a hog with a knife before?" Jake spit into his cup again.

He looked surprised when Tom and I raised our hands.

"Both hunting and on the farm. I only look like I'm city bred," I said. "The boy has helped with slaughtering."

"Yep. He's real people, Jake, he's just got them other professors fooled," Mr. Baker spoke up for me.

"Ah, Mr. Jake. can I visit the dogs?" Tom asked.

"Sure; they're not the most social so don't push it," Jake answered and Tom nodded. He made a beeline for the truck.

"Boy always loved dogs," I said. "No matter how many we have, he's game for more. Let me go wake Frank. He was catching up on sleep."

I woke Frank, then headed back to the porch, and found Mr. Baker and Jake watching the truck. Tom had climbed in the back and had a lap full of dogs, who seemed to be pushing each other out of the way to give him puppy kisses, as some people call face licks.

"I thought you said they weren't that friendly." I heard Mr. Baker say as I headed back.

"They're not. Normally they visit a bit and make it plain, you ain't a pig, they ain't interested." Jake sounded surprised.

"Well, they're sure loving on him," Mr. Baker said.

"He's always been able to charm things," I said.

"Just keep him away from my granddaughters then." Mr. Baker laughed. "I'm too young to be a great grandpa."

While Tommy visited with the dogs, we discussed the plan. Jake and the dogs would start at one end of the river bottom with Frank and Tom. Mr. Baker was going to head down to where the other hunters were staying and fetch those that wanted to come. With a little luck, Jake might make a good bit of money today

They'd follow the dogs through the bottom and see if they could chase up a pig. In deference to my knee, I'd take the mule up to the rise in the middle. It narrowed there and with any luck, the dogs would have found something. The mule would make bringing the carcass back easier.

So Jake, Frank, and Tom piled in the truck, Tom in back with the dogs. As they drove off, I realized Frank might not have a blade. Hopefully Jake had a spare. Otherwise, strangling a pig would be interesting. I knew Tom had a belduque with him. I forged it for him years ago and he pretty much always carried it.

I pulled mine from my bag and stopped to admire the blade. Cable Damascus. Old Steve had made it for me years ago. Before the liver cancer killed him. I carried it since. 11 inches in the old Spanish style that predates the bowie. I added it to the 10mm I always carried in the fields. Minimum I'd trust on an angry pork roast.

I drove to the rise and watched. Jake, Tom, and the group of young men hunting were walking to the bottom. The dogs were bouncing around Jake and the boy until they got a scent. Then things changed. The dogs became very focused and tore off into the bottom. I could hear them baying and pretty soon I heard a panic squeal. Jake urged them on.

I could see the dogs running through the woods, chasing something that was tearing up the ground. Behind them, the hunters followed. Running. Through the trees I saw one slip and fall into the stream. He pulled himself up and hurried after the rest.

The baying intensified and I heard Jake yelling to the dogs.

Then the squealing started as they caught the pig.

"Show 'em how it's done, Tom." Jake hollered.

Following that a large squeal and silent. Well, one coming home.

The hunt continued with the cycle repeating itself a couple times, and they moved nearer to the rise. I had just driven down to the bottom when I heard the baying start, close this time. Huh. I figured by now they were done. As I settled in, a mid-sized sow broke cover and came running full tilt at the mule. Three of the four dogs were in full throat as they chased her.

She saw the mule, tried to turn, but crashed into sideways.

The dogs leapt on her.

I sighed. Drew my knife and hopped down. Dang dogs would tear her apart if I didn't finish this. Grabbing an ear, I stabbed.

Clean. She spasmed and died.

"Damn it, old man, at least try and make it look hard," Frank's voice came to me as I calmed the dogs. It was following by clapping from the other hunters. One said, "Wow, you like didn't even break a sweat, old timer."

I ignored him and looked at Jake and Tom.

"Shit. We don't need any more pork."

"Hunters for the Hungry is still in town," Jake said, referring to the Texas program for getting excess meat to those in need.

"Good, this girl looks like she should be tasty." Then asked Frank, "You get one?

"Yep, nice set of tusks too."

"Cool. Well, let's start cleaning. Coyotes and vultures will take care of the gut piles."

❧

WE CLEANED THE HOGS, AND THEY WERE ALL YOUNG ENOUGH TO BE decent for eating, except Frank's. Tom said that when they routed a big one, Jake let Frank make that kill.

Then, after making sure no one was around, he said, "I don't like it, Dad. It's not really fair with the dogs."

"Yeah, I know, kiddo. However..."

"Oh I know, Dad. It's just we might as well be using a helicopter."

I nodded. I settled up with Jake and slipped him another Benjamin, for this trip made Frank happy and he was a good customer. He needed to get back for a redeye home and Tom offered to drive him. Maddy asked if she could go as she had get home and do some stuff for school. They took off about 6 pm in Monica's car since she planned to spend a couple days with her father. Frank was going to be cutting that 11 pm flight close. Even with the boy driving.

❦

AFTER THEY LEFT, I STAYED ONE MORE NIGHT. NOT REALLY TO HUNT, but to sit in a blind and watch animals. I did that a lot. Hadn't told Frank I didn't even load my rifle this trip. Some Spanish guy said that man kills to prove he hunted, not hunts to kill. Or something like that. I always found it true. Not a lot left to prove at my age. This time I just left the rifle at the house.

I was settling in to watch the dusk fall when I heard a noise near the blind. I waited. One year I had a family of whitetails grazing underneath while I watched. When the door latch rattled, I figured it probably wasn't a deer.

The door opened and Monica slipped in. Coveralls again, light windbreaker over them, cowboy boots, and no hat. Just her hair tied back with a camo ribbon.

"Hey. Thought you might like some company. I brought 'shine."

I raised an eyebrow at that.

"Your gun's at the house. I checked. Noticed your bag was gone too." She gave me a grin and stripped off the jacket before settling into the other chair. I noticed she didn't have the long-sleeved white shirt on this time. Well, it was hot.

I smiled and nodded and she settled in. We sipped companionably and watched the day end.

After a fair bit of watching the sun set and passing the flask back and forth, she asked, "So, professor, what do I need to do to get an A?

17

COUGAR ATTACK BY LA VAUGHN KEMNOW

The dog and the cougar had quite a tussle—but with the help of a well-placed kick by his hiking companion the dog lived.

Our historical research of fire lookouts, while often fulfilling and sometimes stimulating, is not something we consider unduly dangerous. One pleasant early morning hike, however, turned into a spine-tingling adventure for my husband Ron and our little dog Taco.

On Wednesday, July 8, 2009 Ron parked at a locked gate about two or two and a half miles below SiSi Lookout in the Mt. Hood National Forest in northern Oregon, in a never-ending quest for the preservation of Oregon's fire lookout history.

A mile or so up the trail, Ron was startled to hear the dog, a few paces behind him, begin to bark furiously. Ron whirled around to see a cougar in a low crouch, moving rapidly from the thick brush along the trail toward the dog. It soon had little Taco in a firm grip, with the dog's head in the big cat's mouth, shaking him furiously as Taco let out a series of frightened little squeaks.

Having no time to think, Ron shouted in his "best Marine drill sergeant growl," and took a couple of quick steps forward. The cougar then pinned Taco to the ground and just lay there "looking like a little kid who was wondering, can I have this or do I have to give it back?"

With a powerful, well-placed kick to the cougar's head, Ron sent it rolling and the big cat released the dog. Ron said later, "Any NFL team would have been proud of that kick; there was a lot of emotion in it. It was a case of fight or flight—and I wasn't going to run."

The cougar staggered to its feet and went groggily up the hill about twenty feet, where it moved around in slow circles, alternately shaking its head and pawing at its face. Armed with nothing but his hiking boots and a camera, Ron fumbled with the camera for a few seconds, then realized that wasn't a good place to be.

The instant Taco was free he hightailed it back down the road as fast as his short little legs could carry him. Temporarily losing his desire to visit the lookout and wanting to locate Taco, who was his best buddy and constant companion, Ron headed back to the car. Taco was not there, but Ron thought he heard barking up the hill so he retraced his steps for about a half-mile, calling as he went. Not finding the dog, he returned to the car. Still no Taco, so Ron went back up the hill for yet another fruitless search. Thinking his little sidekick was gone forever, he returned to the car and this time Taco was there waiting for him, "wiggling and waggling all over." Ron stated, "I couldn't have been happier to see that little dog waiting by the car."

Taco was treated by a veterinarian for several deep puncture wounds and returned home with drain tubes, stitches, and several medications. He was one sick little dog for a while, but made a full recovery and continued to trot up mountain trails at our heels, anxious to get to the next lookout.

18

WELL, THAT WAS FESTIVE BY LAWDOG

(O*riginally published on the Lawdog Files)*
Back in the late 90s, I was on my first night patrol after having just gotten back from a gun class out of State. Along about 0500 Dispatch called, "Dispatch, Car 12."

The 0500 calls are always interesting, so I admit to some anticipation, "Go ahead."

"1100 Possum Drive, 911 call, report of a possible prowler."

I sighed. 1100 Possum Drive was a nice, middle-aged lady divorcee who called in a prowler about three times a week. Said prowler always being brush rubbing the siding on her house, or a cat, or the wind.

"10-4, en route."

I pulled up in front of the residence, and I can see the Reporting Party in the bay window, still clutching her cordless phone, and pointing frantically to the back of the house.

I admit to a well-concealed sigh, waved at her, and then began making my way around the outside of the house, no doubt to spend several minutes peering into the dark.

Imagine my surprise when I turned the back corner into the back-yard and came nose to snout with a bloody huge feral hog. I remember well — in the middle of that startle-response adrenaline dump — seeing the bristles fly up on his chest. Kind of like he had just gotten centre-punched with a Winchester 127-grain +P+ 9mm. Like the kind I carried in my P7.

And I realize that I was standing in a text-book perfect speed-rock position.

I had just enough time to mentally pat myself on the back, and then the hog (metaphorically-speaking) looked down at the hole in his chest, said (again, metaphorically-speaking), "Oh, you [deleted]", and then headed my way with the obvious intention of adjusting my buttock-to-shoulder-blade ratio.

Not being entirely gormless, my body (not currently admiring the shot that started this whole episode) spun, took two steps, and flung me at the lower limbs of the nearest mesquite tree ... about those two steps ahead of the enraged pig.

So. There I am, hanging like a panicked sloth from the lower limbs by one ankle, one hand, and one wrist, while a Paleolithic-class hog stands below, loudly opining as to my ancestry and sexual proclivities, and daring me to come down.

Yeah, that's not happening. Unfortunately, my current suspended position means I can't get another shot off at the hog without winding up down on terra firma with said ambulatory chop — with him at a decided advantage.

Worse, during the mad sprint for the tree, I seem to have dropped my walkie-talkie.

I resign myself to not going anywhere for a while. A sentiment obviously shared by Senor Puerco.

A lot longer later than I felt was absolutely necessary, I hear the sound of a DPS cruiser pull up outside. At last, think I, back-up. And not before time.

Indeed, back-up soon showed itself cautiously around the corner in the form of the DPS trooper assigned to our wee town. He scans the back-yard with his torch — passing over me the first time, I might add — before the beam settled on the hog. It then panned up.

There were snorting noises that I suspect may have been an attempt to conceal mirth. Not a very good attempt, but at least he tried.

"Shot the hog, didn't you?"

I snarled something that may have been less than courteous, but I plead long-term discomfort.

"I told you that dinky little 9mm wasn't any good, didn't I?"

I was attempting some form of come-back, when I hear the bark of a Texas DPS-issued Sig P220, and the .45 ACP round smacks the hog right behind the foreleg.

I know this, because I had a unique perspective on the second bristle spray of the morning. Which led the hog to announce — at the top of his porcine lungs — "You want a piece of me, too?"

And I watch the DPS trooper scramble to the top of an ancient outhouse with the alacrity and grace of a scalded-arsed ape.

"Nice shot, Tex" I snark from the comfort of my mesquite tree.

"Damn," replied that worthy, "That's a big hog."

I cast a sneer in his general direction, "Why don't you thump it a couple of more times?"

Long pause.

"Can't."

"Well", I snarl, twisting a bit, "I not in any position to do anything about this, so it's pretty much up to you."

The hog sends a grunt my way, letting me know I haven't been forgotten.

This pause is longer. Oh, for the love of ... "You dropped your bang-stick, didn't you?"

"I had something on my mind!" There's another pause, contemplative this time, "I've got my .32 backup."

I can feel a facial tic developing.

This goes on until the sun rises, the hog trots off (with a firmly-cocked snook in our general direction), the trooper and I climb down and solemnly swear to never speak of this again.

Fast-forward about a year, and I'm in Dispatch when the local Game Warden staggers in, and heads for the coffee-pot with the same sort of intensity that a man three days under the Sahara sun heads for an oasis.

"You okay, Harry? I ask, slightly concerned.

"[Deleted] monster hog out by the T bar S," he mutters from around a soothing mug, "Took three rounds from my .450 Marlin. Didn't think the [deleted] was ever going to go down."

I'm mildly impressed. "Damn."

"Checked him over, found this under the skin on his chest." He displays a perfectly-mushroomed Winchester Ranger bullet. Probably about 127 grains, were I to guess, "Some damfool moron shot him with a 9mm sometime. Can you imagine that? Idiot. Some people shouldn't be let out without a minder."

Whoops.

19

BEAR WRASSLIN' BY KERMIT GRENOILLE

Never wrestle a bear.

This aphorism was never expressly stated by Pap, but it was no doubt an assumed piece of advice, essential for Long Life in the Woods (although probably a more boring life to boot, should it be followed). And yet, I watched the old man violate the heck out of it, and well...

My grandfather, or as all the grandkids called him, "Pap," was an old time Appalachian boy who bootstrapped himself through college scholarships, missed the Korean War by a matter of months, and parlayed his USGI benefits (combined with hard work and a nose-to-the-grindstone stick-to-it-iveness that would put a Missouri mule to shame) into two graduate degrees and an illustrious and storied career as a research scientist and college post-graduate studies professor. His professional career spanned projects in at least three continents and more than a dozen different countries, discovering new findings in ruminant toxicology (that's cows and things that poison them for those of us not in his field), developing new techniques for feeding said cows from the most unlikely sources, and teaching and instructing an ever revolving host of graduate students whom he mentored to continue the legacy after he retired. Along the way, he wound up, sometimes almost accidentally, dabbling in international relations with hostile foreign powers, stymying a cocaine importation scheme, and building a Christian campus ministry that persists to this day in two different states at two different universities. But he never lost nor abandoned his country boy roots.

I have told elsewhere the story of my first fishing trip, which he took me on, and that is a tale best retold in the original telling. If you want to read it, go look it up. I'll wait. Well, I won't know if you read it before the rest of this story or afterwards; I'm narrating this one, and you're reading it. How will I know if you took a break? Go for it if you like. I'll be here, one way or another.

Made up your mind? Ok, good. Now on to this little story. All true, by the way, just like the previous one (Or the next, if you read this one first).

Like I said, Pap never lost his Appalachian roots. While an undeniable portion of these roots did indeed include aspects we might consider "redneck" or "hillbilly," far larger was his love for the outdoors. His son, my father, did not share the appreciation of God's Office, but my dad was and is able to appreciate and enjoy others' enjoyment of these things, so I was included in quite a few expeditions and adventures with Pap. One of those was The Cabin.

The year after my first fishing trip, my grandparents purchased a small plot of land in the Sangre del Cristo Mountains, just north of the San Isabel National Forest in Colorado. If you know where Fort Garland or La Veta are, well, that will put you in the right area. Of course I went with them, to "help them pick it out," or some such. That first year, we camped out on a lot bare of anything other than trees and rocks, sleeping in an ancient Scotty travel trailer, and touring the area with Pap's old-but-not-ancient Isuzu Trooper.

A year later, he bought an RV, and I was again invited to go camping. And we visited the land annually in that RV for a few more years before he started building. As I recall, I was an early teenager.

Now, "Grandma's Cabin in Pap's Woods," as he liked to call it, was nothing enormous, nor expensive. It was a simple concrete foundation, wooden construction, with one bedroom, a second floor loft, and some simply huge bay windows facing the southeast. Over time, this cabin would become a meeting place and gathering for the extended family and adopted clan, but...

Pap, having been a child of the Great Depression, and having lived through some hard times of his own, was not a spendthrift. Now, he wasn't averse to spending his own hard-earned money by any means, and he usually kept a handful of twenty dollar bills in his pocket to "pay" his grandchildren for "helping" him with chores. But he was careful in how he spent his money, and he decided that a large portion of the cabin, once frame, floors, and exterior walls were constructed, could in fact be completed by himself. His sons, sons-in-law, and grandsons could help him if he in fact needed help. This did result in a few comedies of error over the next several years, and more than one minor injury, as he essentially had to teach himself home construction, but once it was completed, inside and out, the cabin was quite cozy indeed, and very homey.

From the ground, there was a concrete footer, probably forty feet to a side, with a crawlspace inside it. Above that, wooden siding, carefully treated and stained but retaining its natural grain, no paint. The siding rises to a peaked metal roof, red in color. Most evenings, the central chimney rising from the cast iron stove could be seen pitching its first few puffs of smoke as the last sun rays filtered through the trees to make the bay windows glow in the golden backwash from aspen leaves.

At the back of the second floor loft, there is a small railed balcony, looking back into the trees behind the cabin. It's a perfect spot to sit in the provided chair there for an evening, sipping a last cup of coffee or hot cocoa (added rum or other tipple of choice for those of you of legal drinking age), as you watch the shadows grow long in front of your face, hear the rustle of the sundown wind, and hear the forest switch the sound track from day to night.

Spanning the front of the cabin, facing east and hooking around off to wrap around towards the north side, is an elevated porch, also with a rail. At the front, the porch stands between two and four feet off the ground, and is a handy place to stack firewood to season for the next winter. A grand staircase (well, grand to my way of thought) descends from this porch, immediately in front of the door, and reaches the downsloping driveway below. Around on the side the kitchen door opens to the far end of the porch, with a much smaller set of steps down.

This porch was ground zero for bear wrestling. Or, I should say, "wrassling." Because what occurred on that porch was not only inadvisable, but certainly followed no rules I know of other than simply, "win."

While there were, indeed, other people that lived in this private and gated section of forest, the vast majority of it is considered to be a private game preserve, with no hunting allowed. Many hunters own plots of land within, but they do not load their guns until they have crossed the boundary to the national forest, or they simply go elsewhere. The deer, elk, and various other critters are quite aware of this, too. Within the gates of the community, animals abound.

One family reunion, I was late teens or early twenties, beds were at a premium at the cabin. Some folks parked RVs, some slept on couches, and the floors of the cabin at night were wall to wall sleeping bags and air mattresses. Me, I brought a small tent. One night, I had the strangest dream: something was breathing on my head while it tried to eat my hair. As I was not feeling any teeth upon my scalp, I rolled over and thought nothing of it until the next morning. When I opened my tent flap, though, in the mud and dew were hoof prints of a massive bull elk that had wandered through when the moon was up. It seemed that he had stopped by to investigate the tent, and as my head was pressed against the thin canvas, he took the opportunity to get a really good whiff of my hair through the fabric. Yeah, animals were always close by.

Now, Pap had always made sure to convey the importance of remembering that wild animals are *animals*, and whether predator or prey, they are quite capable of being dangerous under the wrong circumstances. When I was eight, in my first trip in the RV, we traveled through Yellowstone National Park, where I got to witness the incredible stupidity of at least ten or twelve city boy tourists attempting to pet three fully grown bull elk. When he noticed what they were doing, Pap drove off as quickly as possible, muttering something about fools and drunkards before he got too quiet for my young ears to be tarnished by more appropriate language.

At any rate, there were bears in Pap's woods. Quite a few of them. The year that the foundation and framing of the cabin was built, Pap awoke in the middle of the night to some noise coming from the trash can he had tied up in a tree (to keep it away from bears, of course). Upon opening the door, he was immediately faced with a mama bear and two cubs, about twenty yards away, with the tree the can was hung in standing between him and them. And the can moved.

A third cub stuck its head out over the edge of the trash can with a paper plate in its mouth. Now, Pap, knowing as he did that a bear once accustomed to finding food from humans becomes a very dangerous bear indeed, was presented with a problem. He could either close the door and allow Mama and her three cubs to raid the bin, which would likely result in one or more of them breaking into some old lady's house and meeting the business end of a twelve gauge. Or, he could attempt to do something about the bears there and then, at risk to himself from Mama raring up and defending her young, in hopes of sparing the bears' lives later on.

You guessed it. The old man Did Something.

Pap very carefully reached back inside the RV and fetched the broom. Not a regular broom, an RV broom. About three feet long for handy storage. Slowly he unscrewed the head from the handle, placed the bristled end back inside, then stepped off the tiny RV porch to play ringmaster to four bears.

It actually went well. He approached the lee side of the trash can, keeping it between him and Mama, and started bumping the can to set it swinging until the cub's head stuck up again, then poked the baby bear with the handle behind the ear, keeping a careful eye on the big one the entire time. With a bit of swinging and a bit of prodding, he convinced the cub to vacate the bin, yet without causing it to squall or triggering a charge from the mother. Once the cub was out and bouncing back along the ground to its parent, he carefully untied the rope holding the bin up and hoisted it higher up in the tree and hopefully further out of temptation's way. When done (and all very slowly at that, for Mama was still there), he backed back to the RV, stepped back inside, and whooped at the ursine family a couple times to encourage them to leave. Mama Bear and her three littles likewise backed out of the clearing, and the night was quiet.

But that was not Bear Wrassling. Bear Prodding, sure, but not Wrassling. No, that was next year.

Once the cabin was framed up and technically liveable, Pap and Grandma moved in, and I came up for my normal summer stay with them. Now, I say "liveable," but the interior walls were insulation wrapped around studs, the floor was subfloor, and none of the exterior walls or the deck had been sealed yet. So, as was and had been my habit for some years by this point, I helped with what needed done. The day in question, we were painting the deck with a combination stain and sealant.

There have been larger decks made, by persons richer or more pretentious, but the deck painting was still not a one-day job, even for two grown men (well, one grown, and one entering the gangly awkwardness of teenage years). So we took it easy, worked a few hours, took a break, worked a few more hours, then went for a leisurely drive around the dirt roads through the forest, animal spotting.

The second day of porch painting dawned no differently than the first. We got up in the relaxed leisure common only to retirees and teenagers, ate breakfast, donned grubby clothes, and got to work. Just before lunchtime, and as we were ahead of schedule, being about three quarters of the way done, I knocked off early to work on a book I had been reading, and went back inside. Pap stayed outside to finish soaking one last board or three in sealant, while Grandma busied herself from her crossword to fetch sandwich fixings, and I settled on a couch in front of one of the big bay windows overlooking the woods.

After a couple minutes, I noticed something odd. There was banging coming from the kitchen side of the porch. Grandma was clearly visible inside, and looking over my shoulder, I could see Pap through the window. And yet, there was A Noise, and then I saw the trashcan wobble.

Now, Pap had, up to this point, had the trash bins up on the porch over by the kitchen door, for ease of disposal and transportation to the transfer station. Fewer steps that way. His compromise to the wildlife was to batten the lids down fast on each can with those heavy solid rubber bungee cords, one per side handle to handle across the top, and then bungeed the whole thing to the porch railing.

But one can was moving. And clearly NOT still bungeed to the rail. I stood up.Looked at Grandma in the kitchen.Looked at the bear dragging the can off the porch. Looked back at Pap. Looked at the...

"Pap! There's a bear in the garbage!"

If anyone ever thinks that with old age comes decrepitude, you have never met my grandfather. If you had, you would be forever disabused of the notion. Once you met him, you never forgot him, for a great many reasons, not least of which was the display of nimbleness and strength that old man displayed.

My seventy-plus-year-old Pap jumped up from his painting, dropping the brush only God and John Denver knew where, sprinted around the outside of the cabin, and slammed up against the railing by the porch steps just in time to snag one handle of the trash bin with one hand, the other gripping the corner post of the steps. It probably took him three seconds, tops, to process and react.

Thankfully, it was not a large bear. In fact, it was a yearling cub. Likely the same cub he had chased out of the same trash can the year previous. Now weaned and kicked out by Mama, the bear had returned to a place he remembered as easy picking for a quick snack. So he was not large by any means. But he weighed as much as Pap did, at least, and he had four paw drive. Pap... had West Virginia wiriness, honed and polished from a lifetime of hard work and hunting. It was a bit of a stalemate.

Picture a mostly still wet from sealant porch. An old man with his left hand in white-knuckled grip on a trash can handle, right hand planted on a wooden 4x4 fixed to concrete, right foot on the decking proper, left foot down a step or two. Picture a half grown bear, teeth firmly embedded in the trash can lid, both front paws on the bottom step, rear legs throwing dirt from the ground. Both are pulling, yanking, giving a moment, then dragging the other, in a tug of war over a garbage can containing some paper plates smelling of bacon grease.The old man is yelling at the bear, the bear is growling at the old man, and neither is gaining much advantage either way. The tug of war went on for at least half a minute like that, possibly more.

And then Pap got tired of the stalemate.

Letting go of the porch railing, but not the can, he allowed himself to get dragged down the steps, giving himself just enough momentum... and as his right foot hit terra firma, his left came off the bottom step with the full force of both his and the bear's body weights pulling him forward, and planted a kick right in that bear's ribcage.

WHUUUUUFFFFFFFF!!!!!

The bear instantly abandoned his pursuit of tasty chicken leftovers, released the trashcan, and took off back into the tree line. You remember those old cartoons, where a running character had spinning dervishes instead of legs? Yeah, it was kinda like that.

Pap stood there still holding the garbage can, panting and sweating from exertion, shook his left leg out, and turned around to see me still frozen agog in the kitchen door at the display of sheer mountain man muleheadednness I had just witnessed.

"Boy, if I ever catch you doing something as colossally stupid as what I just did, I'll....!"

Trailing off, he refastened the can to the porch rail, and went inside to eat a sandwich and have a cold soda.

Oh, the bear was fine. Two weeks later, we ran him off again, and Pap moved the trashcans to the upstairs balcony where it couldn't reach.

❧ 20 ❧

SPRITE BY KELLY GRAYSON

November, 1988

    My eyes snap open, and I stare at the ceiling for a moment as I try to get my bearings. It doesn't take long. A chorus of gentle snoring reverberates in each ear, accompanied by warm breath on my neck. I turn my head to the left, and the warm breath is replaced by a cold, wet nose prodding gently. I'm home in bed, and it's...

... 4:27 am. Damn, time to wake up.

    I don't bother to turn my head away. There will only be another cold wet nose over there, and that one licks, too. Instead, I roll out of bed and pad over to my stereo and turn it off. After years of sleeping through alarm clocks, I have finally discovered something that works: put my stereo on an appliance timer, and turn the volume to ten. After a week of being rudely yanked from my slumber by the local rock station, and not a few angry complaints from my neighbors at the marina, I find myself waking several minutes before my alarm goes off. It's a powerful thing, conditioning.

    I turn back to the bed. Sprite is already up, sitting inquisitively on the edge of the bed, head cocked, regarding me intently. For her part, Jazz lifts a lazy head from the pillow, blinks balefully at both of us, and plops her head back onto the pillow. She grumbles, deep in her throat, in what any dog person would recognize as disgust.

"Morning people," is the human translation, and I know that she's grumbling about Sprite, not me. Were it not for the puppy, and the day it is, Jazz and I would still be in bed, safely ensconced beneath the covers until well after daybreak.

"What's with the innocent look?" I grunt at Sprite, mockingly stern. "You chew another gun stock while I was asleep?" Her ears droop, and her head lowers.

"It's okay, Sprite," I chuckle, leaning over with my hands on my knees. "I'm not mad anymore. Nor am I mad about my belt, my boots, the couch leg, the rug by the door..."

By way of reply, Sprite launches herself from the bed like a released spring, landing on the back of my head and shoulders. Her momentum carries her over my back and onto the counter behind me, where she scrabbles madly for footing before tumbling in an ungainly heap on the floor.

"Dog," I laugh aloud, shaking my head in consternation, "either you're going to learn some house manners soon, or we're both going to need sedatives."

Sprite ignores me, madly dashing around my studio apartment in a headlong, adrenaline-fueled pinball circuit of destruction. Her path takes her to the back door, turning over her food bowl as she goes, across my desk chair, a kamikaze leap to the couch, off the arm of the couch to the front door, pausing just long enough to growl fiercely and bark at my waders and blind bag, around behind my knees, whacking the open door to the stereo cabinet, and then to the back door again... the loop gets ever faster, and ever more haphazard, finally culminating with a leap onto the bed, skidding in a tangle of bedcovers right into...

... Jazz, who with a flash of teeth and a menacing snarl, calms the puppy down as well as I could ever hope. Cowed, Sprite hops from the bed and bounds over to me, hoping to find a more willing playmate.

"Don't look at me," I laugh. "I'm barely awake myself." I can't fault the pup for being rambunctious. After all, she comes from a long line of forebears carefully bred for generations to be all gas, no brakes. That's the way I like 'em.

Tail wagging furiously, Sprite crouches in front of me, hind legs coiled, the muscles bulging under her glossy black coat. Even at four months old, she's got the body of a conditioned athlete. Long and lean, hugely muscled haunches, face narrower and more refined than the classic block head of the show-bred Labs, her lines bespeak generations of careful breeding for desirable physical traits and temperament. She is built for function, not looks.

Her pedigree is littered with all the iconic names in field trialing; Choice, Cadillac Mack, Cody, Honcho... heck, if you go back far enough, even Super Chief. Whether she'll ever realize her potential is another story. She'll have a long way to go just to equal Jazz...

... who, come to think of it, never realized her potential, either. I watch as she slowly crawls out of bed, creeping forward until she can put her front feet on the floor, then dragging her withered hindquarters off the bed behind her, almost as an afterthought.

It was a training accident, right before her fourth birthday. They said she'd never walk again, but they didn't know Jazz. As it was, we had to retire her from active competition, but that didn't stop her from being the hottest retriever in any man's duck blind. Even at half-speed, she was faster than most.

I grimace as I watch her hobble to the door. The hitch in her stride was less painful to watch back when I knew it didn't cause her pain. Now, I'm not so sure. Sprite, seeing Jazz up and about, takes it as an invitation to play, and focuses her disgustingly fresh, early-morning puppy energy on the older dog. Jazz growls warningly, but Sprite pays no heed. Her pinball circuit starts anew, with Jazz as its epicenter.

I let her romp for a bit, willing to put up with a little rambunctiousness, until she collides with Jazz, knocking her over.

All right, enough.

"*SIT!*" I bellow fiercely, my anger surprising us both. Sprite screeches to a halt and plants her ass on the tile with an audible *thump*. Jazz, smart enough to know I'm not angry with her, just scrambles laboriously to her feet and hobbles to the door. I open the door and let her outside, watching her squat in the grass, just off the flagstones.

Barely made it outside this time. Damn.

Behind me, Sprite is still sitting, frozen in the same position. Her ears are laid flat against her skull, her head lowered in submission. She briefly looks at me, and then glances away, nervously licking her chops.

"It's okay, Sprite," I sigh, adopting a gentler tone. I kneel in front of her, taking her head in my hands and pressing my forehead to hers. I scratch her roughly behind the ears and cuff her on the head gently. She responds by licking my face and gently nipping at my hand.

"All right, dog," I chuckle, getting up and pointing to the open door. "Go do your business."

Happily, she bounds outside after Jazz, skidding around the privacy fence and disappearing from sight. Shaking my head, I shut the door behind her and go through my gear one last time. Hip boots, blind bag, gun, duck calls, honey buns, plenty of shells...everything is as it should be.

Well, almost everything.

On second thought, I remove one box of shells from my bag and put them back in my gear locker. I'm not going to be shooting that much this morning, anyway. I dig through the assorted detritus on the bottom shelf of the locker, finally find what I was looking for, and stash it in the side pocket of my blind bag.

Ten minutes later, I'm dressed, and I quickly fill my Thermos with hot water from my coffeemaker and dump in double the recommended number of packets of instant cocoa. I'm the only guy I know who has a coffeemaker, who doesn't drink coffee. Works great for heating water for hot chocolate, though. A chorus of barking dogs tells me that Jazz and Sprite have woken the others, and I quickly step out the back door to silence the racket.

When my brother owned this place, he did it with one whistling crack of a bullwhip. Me, I prefer to let the tone and volume of my voice do the same thing. If he were here, he might say that it's easier to quiet six dogs than twenty, but I have my own way of doing things.

And soon enough, my own way of doing things will have all these kennels filled again, and I still won't need a bullwhip to quiet the barking, because I'm better than Terry was. At least, that's what I tell myself. My brother may disagree, but more likely he'd say that the comparison is pointless. I'm supposed to be taking the MCAT and applying to medical schools right now, not playing Peter Pan trying to revive a failed business with a has-been dog and a never-was puppy.

My career choice isn't a popular one with my family right now, but that's okay with me. My family hasn't been popular with *me* for years. The only thing that hurts is the distance between me and my brother. I'm used to being the arrogant brother to my sisters, or the cold and distant son my parents thought they had.

What I'm not used to is being a disappointment to my brother. He practically raised me. I would have thought he knew me better.

But that's okay too, I tell myself. Today is the opening day of duck season, 1988, and for the first time since I was thirteen, I'm at peace with my life. I'm going duck hunting this morning, and all is right with the world.

Well, *almost* everything.

Because today, also for the first time since I was thirteen, I'm going hunting without Jazz.

She was more than just a showcase dog. She was a family pet, like Roxy and Velvet before her, but Jazz was the first one with the potential to win championships. She was supposed to be the one that made Terry's career, that one that brought him recognition as a top trainer.

All those hopes ended in a leap off a tall bank in Escalon, California, in the summer of '85. When she came home, she wasn't the same dog, and Terry wasn't the same man.

Or perhaps he was, and I had never really known him, either. One way or the other, his dreams of a career withered along with Jazz's legs, having given up on dog training long before he officially closed the doors of this place.

He enrolled in college, discovering his talent for prose, taking the same joy from shaping words into ideas that he'd once taken from molding a raw puppy into a polished hunter. He'd be a writer one day, and perhaps after the publication of his third or fourth novel, he'd take a faculty position at the university as a writer in residence. Or write more novels. He had the talent.

For a brief time, we were both students at the same university; he majoring in English literature, me in biology. We were never closer, and I had no doubt that he was proud of his little brother.

All that ended when I dropped out of school.

I started working Jazz again, entered her in a few hunting retriever tests, and re-opened this place. Six months later, I bought Sprite, having realized that if I was going to make a name for myself in this sport, it wasn't going to be with a dog someone else had trained – even if everything I knew about dog training I had absorbed while watching her develop. You might even say we went to school together, Jazz and I.

One day, perhaps I'll go back to school. I'll finish up my junior year, take the MCAT, find a medical school somewhere. I'll be a doctor, and perhaps then my brother the writer will speak to me again.

Then again, maybe he won't. Maybe I won't speak to him, because, well... *fuck him*. I'm good at this, and if he can't be proud of me for that, then I don't need his love or his approval. I've got the love of his dog, and that's all I need. *Her* loyalty is not fickle.

Jazz has been there for every hunt, every field trial, every training session, and she's never let me down – even when she's embarrassed me in public. You can't blame the Ferrari when you're not enough driver to handle her properly, after all.

Outside, she's romping in the yard with her successor. They've found a training bumper somewhere, and Jazz is playing keep away from Sprite, keeping her at bay with guile and, when necessary, sheer intimidation. Jazz is still the Alpha bitch at this kennel, and every dog here knows it.

I briefly toy with the notion of bringing her along again. Looking at her now, it's obvious she still has plenty of steam, and God knows I'd rather not bring a green puppy, barely obedience trained and not yet even steady to wing and shot, to the blind on opening day...

... but it's not now that I'm thinking of, but later. Later, after a full day of hunting, even in weather as mild as late November, when the day will end with me carrying my dog to the truck because she's too weak to climb in by herself, having left everything she had in the duck blind. Later, when she'll lie on the couch like a dead thing, too tired to even get down to eat. Later, when every move will bring a painful yelp, made all the more wrenching for me knowing that, if I asked, she'd be back in the blind the next morning.

As much as I love my dog, I'll not ask that of her again, even if it means facing my betrayal in her eyes as I leave her behind.

And so I paw through my blind bag yet one more time, taking longer to hose down the kennels than it should, schlepping my gear to the truck with all the enthusiasm of a misbehaving child sent to the hedge to pick his own switch.

When I open the truck door, Sprite leaps in effortlessly, skidding across the seat into the passenger door with a thump. Jazz aims lower, for the floorboards, and still manages to drag her legs on the sill as she gets in.

"Not today, Jazz," I say softly, hating myself for the catch in my voice. "Come on girl, let's go back inside." I snap my fingers and turn to go, but she doesn't follow. She's still sitting in the floor of my truck, looking at me with confusion.

Don't make me do it this way, Jazz. Please.

"Jazz. *Heel*," I command more firmly, taking her collar and dragging her gently out of the truck. With leaden heart I lead her back to the office and lock her inside, assiduously avoiding the look in her eyes as the door closes in her face.

Sprite tentatively nuzzles my face as I climb back into the truck, licking at the salty tears gathering at the corner of my eyes. "Little one," I sigh warningly as I start the truck, "you better be friggin' spectacular today."

IN DUCK HUNTING PARLANCE, I'M A MUDPUPPY, ONE OF THOSE GUYS that spends the majority of his time hunting flooded rice fields. I hunt in far northeast Louisiana, close enough to the state line that a heart-shot cripple can, and often does, lock his wings and sail into Arkansas. The fields I hunt belong to a training client, the owner of Sprite's littermate, in fact. This early in the season, he and his buddies will be hunting other fields, proven blinds that produce a lot of birds. This blind is brand new, and I have the entire place to myself.

It's a bit different than I'm used to, this being a mudpuppy. There are no flooded river bottoms, no rafts of acorns carpeting the water beneath a quiet cathedral of pin oaks, no pre-dawn runs up the river into the teeth of a north wind, navigating the fog-shrouded channel by the dim glow of a bow light. Compared to carefully wading the cypress sloughs, where every submerged root threatens to make you float your hat, sitting in a dry pit blind seems almost like cheating.

On the other hand, I have an unfettered view of the horizon, where the plum-colored bruise of night sky fades slowly to pink, and God whispers words of healing hidden in the whistling of wings overhead. There is a moment – just a brief one, but nonetheless profound for all its brevity – in the pre-dawn stillness where the stars and the sun coexist in the same sky, where the stars wink their goodbyes over one shoulder while the sun bids me good morning with a kiss of warmth on the other.

You don't get that view in the flooded timber. Dawn in the river bottoms comes like turning up a rheostat, where the darkness fades from all directions, showing you at first the spectral image of the canopy above you, slowly bringing the trees into stark relief, and then suddenly it's just... *daylight.* It's almost as if, instead of a gentle wash from starlight to sunrise, God instead calls reveille, His bugle the thunder of guns in the distance and the screech of wood ducks through the timber.

Either way, if I don't hurry, I'm going to miss it.

I park my truck in front of the camp, hustle my gear over to the four-wheeler, and fire it up. Sprite noses around the yard, investigating new smells, and I call her over and pat the rear cargo rack. *"Kennel,"* I command, and obediently she loads up, installing herself in Jazz's customary position, standing on the rack behind me, chest pressed against my back and head resting on my shoulder as we hurtle down the farm roads toward my blind, dust clouds billowing in our wake. Give it another six weeks, and those dust clouds will be replaced by rooster tails of mud from beneath my tires, and the trip will seem twice as long. Biting January winds tend to do that to boat runs and ATV rides.

An abandoned tractor tire overgrown with weeds looms out of the darkness, and a rabbit bolts down the road, just at the edge of my headlights. Sprite shifts her weight behind me, and, too late, I hit the brakes. She bails off the ATV in one fluid leap, in hot pursuit of the darting cottontail.

"NO, HERE!" I bellow, and reluctantly she abandons the chase, casting a longing glance over her shoulder as if to say, *"Aww, you're no fun."*

"Ducks, not rabbits," I tell her sternly, patting the cargo rack behind me. "Now load up."

Obediently, she jumps up behind me, but I can tell from her body language that she'd rather run than ride. Her muscles are corded with tension, and she's teetering on the fine edge of balance, ready to jump at the first cue from me that such a leap will be tolerated.

Oh, what the hell. Let her run alongside. Sprinting the rest of the way to the blind might take some of the edge off anyway.

"Fine," I sigh resignedly as I slow down yet again. I lean to my right, out of her way, and wave at the darkness around us. "Go play!"

I barely have *"play"* past my lips before she launches herself off the ATV, snuffling around in the tall weeds on the edge of the dusty road. I pull away, slowly at first until I know she's following, then picking up speed. She keeps pace with me all the way to the blind, muscles rippling beneath her glossy coat, not even breathing hard. Her stride is long, fluid, effortless. The damned dog can probably run thirty miles an hour for another couple of miles.

But the blind is right here, not three hundred yards down the side levee. I stop the Honda in the weeds alongside the road, and quickly begin unloading gear. Legal shooting time is only minutes away, and we're running behind. Sprite finally notices that she's in a race by herself, and circles back, running circles around me as I hustle to the blind.

I drop my gear in the weeds at the water's edge, clamber down into the pit, and pull my 870 in after me. Blind bag comes in next, stowed on the bench seat beside me, and finally I call to Sprite. She's been investigating the decoy spread while my attention was diverted, and favors me with a muddy rice field shower as she shakes the water from her coat. Grimacing and wiping my face with one hand, I snap the D ring in her collar to the chain welded to the front wall of her dog box.

I hastily load my shotgun and sit the rest of the box of steel shot on the shelf that runs the length of the blind. My 870's barrel fits into one of the notches cut into the front lip of that shelf, and my Thermos cup of hot chocolate goes right next to my shells. I dig a honey bun out of my blind bag, take a couple of bites, and hold the rest out for Sprite. She regards the treat impassively for a few moments, and then, like a striking snake, snaps the rest of the honey bun out of my hand and inhales it in one gulp. No matter how many times I've seen her do it, I still can't get used to seeing a dog move so fast.

As the horizon starts to pinken over my right shoulder, I pull the blind flaps closed, and dig through my blind bag for the item I stashed in there as an afterthought this morning. I sit it carefully on the shelf in front of me, taking care not to spill its contents, and reach up to scratch Sprite's ears as we both listen to the world awaken around us.

"Birds oughta be coming soon, little one," I whisper. "I hope you're ready for this."

Sprite answers with a shudder and a soft whine, and rests her muzzle on my left shoulder as we face East, watching God paint the sky though a curtain of dewy spider webs and switch cane.

The only thing missing is Jazz.

THE FIRST DUCK OF THE MORNING TAKES US BY SURPRISE, THE whistling of wings overhead the only warning of his approach. He glides over the blind from right to left, almost close enough to touch, swinging past the edge of my decoy spread and hooking back sharply into the wind before I can even raise the call to my lips. A few flat, atonal quacks identify him as a drake gadwall, and his feet barely touch water before I throw the flaps and shoulder my 870.

There is an infinitesimal moment of recognition between us as he realizes his mistake, knows the black, shadowy square on the levee for what it is. It may be opening day of duck season in Louisiana, but these ducks have been shot at, and called to, all the way from the prairies of Manitoba. By the time they get to the mouth of the Mississippi flyway, there are few stupid ones left.

The moment runs by in slow motion as his wings flare and beat downward in one powerful thrust, the gray primary feathers seemingly pushing the water away in twin depressions, one on either side, launching him from the surface of the water as if spring-loaded, trailing droplets of silver behind him as he claws for altitude, a second wing beat, then a third and a fourth...

... until he rises above the skyline, secondary feathers glowing like angel wings in the waxing dawn. I pick him up with the barrel, the front bead a hazy afterthought as I swing through and pull...

... and just like that he crumples, my slide runs back and forward again, spitting out the empty hull in a brilliant green arc and bringing another 1 ¼ ounces of steel #4 shot back into battery. My ears report the hollow clatter of the empty brass against the steel wall of the blind a full second before gravity reclaims the drake in a mighty splash. I stand there with my gun at port arms, replaying the moment in my mind as I watch the first duck of the season bob belly-up in the decoys, waiting for my dog to...

... Shit, I forgot to tell Sprite to mark. Did she even see that?

A glance to my left tells me I needn't have worried. Sprite is locked in, ears cocked forward, staring intently at the dead gadwall on the water. She shifts her weight forward slightly, rising off her haunches until the chain fastened to her collar reminds her that, no, it is not time to go. She whines softly and sits back down.

"Sit," I say softly, more reminder than command, simply taking advantage of another opportunity to associate the word with the action. Smiling, I watch her for a few moments, then unclip the snap from the D ring on her collar. She remains motionless, a glossy black statue in profile, cocked and waiting for release.

"Sprite," I say softly, and before the sibilant *"esss"* passes my lips, she is in the air, launching herself up and out of the sunken dog box, her own miniature pit blind welded onto the side of mine. One more bound, and she's in the water and swimming, paddling so hard her front shoulders rise a couple inches out of the water. She lets out an exuberant little yip a split second before she reaches the dead gadwall.

Twenty seconds later and she's back, and the sky is filling with birds. If I were hunting with Jazz, I'd stay in the blind and keep calling, trusting her to step back down into the dog box on her own and deliver the bird to hand. There have been many occasions when Jazz marked the fall of more ducks while still holding the bird from the last retrieve in her mouth.

But she ain't Jazz, and she's not even force-fetched yet. Better get out there and get the bird from her, Kelly.

But I barely have my foot on the first rung welded onto the side of the blind before Sprite is there. She steps into the dog box, sits down, and cranes her head over the inner wall of the blind, whining softly around the bird in her mouth.

"Good girl," I croon approvingly as I take the gadwall from her. I try to scratch her ears, but she snatches her head back impatiently, facing forward and scanning the sky eagerly as if to say, "Let's dispense with the praise and the petting, mmmkay? There's *birds* out there!"

Chuckling, I scan the sky and pick out a group of eight mallards to my right, squinting to pick them out against the rising sun. I put my call to my lips and blow a highball; eight loud, raspy and, hopefully, inviting notes.

The group seems to stagger in midair, and then, the back five peel off and circle around behind the blind, sliding along the levee a hundred yards behind the blind before swinging downwind to my left. I call again, just a few plaintive, insistent notes, the mallard hen equivalent of *"Helloooo, sailor!"*

I watch them turn, 200 yards out, working their way upwind inexorably back to my decoys, when an unexpected shadow flashes overhead and I hear the distinctive *"Zzzzzrrreeeep,"* of a drake mallard.

I freeze and cast my eyes upwards, right, left, desperately searching for the birds that just buzzed the blind. Were anyone else there to see it, they might say I look like a demented Jack Nicholson, with a major crick in his neck.

Well looky here, it's the other three from that bunch! Welcome back!

The drake I heard calling is out front, over the decoys, heading swiveling this way and that as he searches for that tart little hen he heard calling to him so seductively just a few moments ago. If I wanted, I could toy with them a bit more, probably light the whole bunch in the decoys. Were it any other day, with my other dog, I'd probably do it.

But today it's just me and Sprite, and she needs easy single retrieves, not the temptation of a dozen live birds swimming in the decoys thirty feet away. I throw the flaps, shoulder my 870 and swing on the drake, who at that moment had decided to light in the decoys and had his wings cupped and feet extended in preparation to do just that.

The sudden movement in front of him changes his mind, however, and I wait for him to climb out of my decoys before I put the bead on his breast and pull, sending him tumbling over backward in a cascade of white feathers. He lands at the outside edge of my decoy spread, thirty-nine yards away. I know it's thirty-nine yards exactly, because he's currently flapping around right next to the snow goose decoy I placed there as a range marker.

I do a lot of shooting during duck season, and I hold to the belief that magnum shells and heavier shot charges are not as effective as consistently putting the shot string into the same patch of sky as the duck. I shoot 2 ¾ inch shells, and I don't take any shots beyond forty yards, period. Usually, the ranges are not even half that.

I cast a glance at Sprite to find her locked on, watching the drake intently. I reach to unclip the snap from her collar and...

... damn, she's not even latched in. And yet she's rock steady. Little one, you are certainly full of surprises.

"Sprite!" I bark sharply, and just like the first retrieve, her release command has barely passed my lips before she's in the water and swimming strongly. I watch her close on the drake, only to see the duck flip over in the last ten feet and dive beneath the surface.

Sprite pulls up in confusion, swimming in circles where she had last seen the drake. She whines and yips in frustration. I start to get out of the blind but change my mind.

No, let's see how she handles it. Unless he grabs hold of a root and stays down, he'll pop up close by. Let's see if she can find him.

Sprite mills around uncertainly, whining softly, when the duck pops up in the open water, twenty feet away. She sees him come up, and takes off after him, kicking her swimming into a gear I didn't know she had. When she's barely three feet away, the duck dives again.

Sprite yips in frustration.

Okay Kelly, you're expecting too much of a four-month-old puppy. Get your ass out of the blind and help your dog.

I sigh and grab a handful of marbles from the pouch I had stashed in my blind bag before I left the office; a contingency plan I had hoped I'd never use. By the time I've climbed out of the blind and fetched my 870, Sprite is back in the decoys, swimming in confused circles. She mouths a teal decoy, eager to bring something, *anything*, back to the blind.

"*NO, drop!*" I call out, and she releases the teal block and resumes her frustrated yipping. The drake pops up twenty yards behind her, still in open water. On her second circle, she sees it and takes off in pursuit. Again, the bird teases her by diving when she's barely three feet away.

I'll just shoot the damned thing again the next time it pops up.

Before I get the chance, the drake pops up just a few feet from Sprite's left shoulder. She's turning right, her predator's eyes focused forward, but something must have alerted her to its presence, because she immediately reverses course and lunges like a striking snake. The hapless drake has no more chance to escape than the honey bun she inhaled this morning.

She emerges from the water growling fiercely, holding the drake at the base of one wing as he furiously wing-whips her with the other. I chuckle as I gently pry the bird from her jaws, and for the first time, she acts like the inexperienced puppy she is. As I pull the bird away, she grabs the drake again, eager to play tug o' war.

"*Drop it,*" I command firmly, pinching her mouth, just above her molars. Surprised, she spits the bird out and sits down, looking at me intently. This is delicate ground I tread, hunting with a puppy not yet force-fetched. I have precious little control over her, like trying to drive a Porsche with no brakes. Downshifting will slow you down only so much.

I turn my back to Sprite, carefully wring the drake's neck, and holding it along with my 870 in my right hand, take Sprite's collar in my left hand and point her toward the dog box.

"*Kennel,*" I command.

She does.

"*Sit.*"

She does.

I reach down and snap her collar to the chain in the dog box before I climb back into the blind. She's too young and too inexperienced to be trusted. And on top of that, she ain't Jazz.

"*You ain't Jazz,*" I tell her loudly, surprising both of us with the spiteful accusation in my tone.

. . .

MORE BIRDS COME, AND MORE BIRDS ARE FELLED, AND SPRITE PICKS them up with all the aplomb of a seasoned hunter. I take singles only, taking only the shots that would result in an easy fall, our front in the decoys. In between, I call to plenty of birds, even lighting a couple big groups of mallards in the decoys for minutes at a time. Sprite watches them with laser-like focus, yet sits so still, so placidly, that she may as well be carved from obsidian.

In the same situation, Jazz would have remained steady, but she'd have quivered and shook and whined, her desire to retrieve a barely caged thing, threatening to erupt at any second like steam from a pressure cooker. In contrast, Sprite's line manners are impeccable. She never even rattles the chain snapped to her collar. She just waits, like a cocked hammer. There is no sense of the power she holds in reserve.

That is, until you trip the sear.

The last bird of the day is a lone pintail drake, a big bull sprig warily scoping out the decoys as if he suspects something is amiss. As pintails are wont to do, his first pass is the lowest, with each successive swing over the decoys progressively higher, until he's on the ragged edge of shooting range.

Still, he turns every time I call. As long as he keeps looking, there may yet arise a chance to scratch him out of the sky. Every time he's overhead, every time I'm looking at anything but his tail growing ever smaller, I will myself to remain perfectly still, tracking his flight only by moving my eyes. I track him as he swings downwind until he leaves my field of vision, then tuck my chin into my right shoulder and wait to pick him up in my peripheral vision as he swings back around.

On a couple of those passes, I notice Sprite doing the same thing. You can't teach a dog such things, and I highly doubt she's mimicking me. It's just something a dog either knows, or doesn't.

Apparently, Sprite just knows.

After five minutes of interminable teasing, I make up my mind to shoot. As the pintail swings from left to right over the outer edge of the decoys, I mount my shotgun and pick him up with my bead. He's tall... so impossibly tall... sixty yards if he's an inch. I swing through his streamlined, graceful head, one bird length, then two before I pull the trigger...

... and he staggers in midair, then starts to claw for altitude. I rack the slide, maintain my lead, and pull again. Shoot a third time, and lower the gun to port arms, staring as he wings away.

"Sorry, dog," I apologize, looking over at Sprite. "It won't be the last time I let you down with my shooting." She ignores me, still staring at the departing pintail, then breaks her silence with a soft whine, and her ears raise another notch.

I look over my shoulder to see the pintail over the far edge of the field, wings locked and rapidly losing altitude. I gape, open-mouthed, as he splashes down in the far corner of the field and lies motionless on the surface.

Damn, talk about the Golden BB! And Sprite marked the fall...

I unclip the chain from Sprite's collar and send her for the bird. Without even a glance to see which way she's headed, I pack up my shells, screw the cap back on my Thermos, and unload my 870. I toss my blind bag onto the top of the blind, hang the birds on a duck strap and toss into onto the roof as well, and climb out of the blind.

By the time I've slung my shotgun and turned around, Sprite is halfway across the field, swimming unerringly toward the downed pintail. It's over 400 yards to the corner of that field, and the sunlight on the water almost renders the bird invisible at dog's-eye level. Still, she's swimming as true as if she were on rails.

I watch her, musingly, for a few more seconds. Then I fish around in my pockets, kneel down and reach into the blind, and with no small amount of satisfaction, put each and every marble back into the pouch and leave them there on the shelf.

Looks like I may not need them after all.

❧ 21 ❧
WHY WE HUNT BY KAT STEVENS

As much as I love reliving the "oh, crap" moments of hunts, there's some serious depth to the reason many of us hunt. Me, I came from a no-guns and no-hunting family, which is just one reason I adore my gun-toting, skilled family of choice today. How I got into hunting involves a combination of reading Elmer Keith's column in old magazines my best friend's dad had when I was a kid and a major passion for all things meat. Combining meat with firearms with time in the woods sounds like an excellent way to spend time.

We all do it, teasing friends about the flood of sunset and sunrise photos on social media, with no BBD or lineup of ducks in sight. But... isn't that kind of what most of us really love? Sure, the rush of a perfect shot on a gorgeous ten-point buck—or my personal best, a 17-point atypical—is unparalleled, but there's so much more to it.

I'm here to tell you that going out hunting isn't about trophies or being cool, it's about the experience. Where else can you sit in silence, enjoying the magenta and royal blue streaks of the sunrise, with no interruptions? Do you often get to enjoy a morning travel mug of coffee while breathing in clean, fresh air with the only sounds around you being made by birds and the sinister squirrels who like to make you think a monster buck is on its way?

Hunting is a tradition I'm passing on to my kids. Bear with me, this has a point—and there's a story coming.

When I was a teenager, it seemed like a brilliant plan to marry young. Then Grace happened, and I knew full well what an awful idea it was to be married to an abusive man (I swear, this story has a happy ending). This lead to the expected, cliched years of struggle as a single mom, the financial woes, the attending of parent-teacher conferences all by my lonesome. However, it also lead to teaching my daughter to shoot, hunt, and process meat. How many people can say their now-19-year-old daughter could go out and shoot a hog or deer—or whatever—and cook it up? How many people have teenage daughters who manage to outshoot a lot of guys in a handgun class? Oh, and how many people have a teenage daughter doing Second Amendment political art for a popular, well-known gun website?

That'd be me.

This isn't all about her, though. As amazing as Grace is, I decided it was a great plan to have an 18 year age gap between kids.

That's how this is the story of Beau.

I met my husband on a hunt. Actually, we met years before we ever started seeing one another. Sometimes I think of those wasted years of total ignorance of what could be and I get irritated at myself. But eventually, fate stepped in, and my favorite hunting partner became the guy who is stuck with me for life (sorry, Dusty). And then there's Beau.

With an 18 year age gap you might think it would be exhausting to raise a toddler, and you'd be right. He is barely over 1 year old as I write this, but there have already been a ridiculous moment of hunting memories.

Beau was 6 days old the first time we took him hunting. The prey in question was feral hogs, because that's what we could hunt in the spring in North Texas. It was a little complicated because I was worn out and Beau was too tiny for ear pro. We made it happen anyway. In the end, Beau and I waited back by the truck while my husband, Dusty, stalked a sounder of hogs. He ended up shooting a big spotted sow, and the resulting photograph of proud dad and 6-day-old Beau will probably be a favorite of mine for years to come. You see, if anyone could possibly be born with hunting in his blood, it's Beau.

At a little over a year of age, Beau has been on dozens of hog hunts, at least twenty deer hunts, a handful of random bird hunts, and quite a few fishing trips on the boat. In the beginning, we went out as a family. Beau would curl into a teensy, sleeping ball of newborn cuteness on Dusty's or my chest and we'd sit and watch the fields. We were all too tired for an active hunt, and a baby made it harder, so truck hunting became a thing.

When deer season rolled around, I knew it was time to start hunting on my own...with Beau. The only way we'd tag out would be to divide and conquer, and we really did and do need the meat.

Here's how we know Beau is destined to be an obsessed hunter. Early in deer season, Dusty got lucky and dropped a narrow-racked buck that was big, but strange looking. When he brought it home, I carried Beau outside to check it out. At that point Beau had only seen hogs and does, so this was something new.

He reached out shaky baby hands and grabbed antlers for the first time. And his face lit up like Christmas morning. A look of glorious excitement came over him, and I knew, at that moment, he'd be chasing deer the rest of his life.

A month or so later, I dropped a buck while he was with me in the truck, which gave him another chance to touch antlers. This time he gave me a look of wonder, tapping and touching the sun-bleached bone of a buck that would soon be made into dinner.

And yes, he loves venison. In fact, he's loved every kind of game meat he's tried.

I know what you're thinking: "Well, this isn't funny at all!" No, it isn't.

In just one year, I've built a treasure trove of hunting memories with my son. From the first time he touched antlers to the moment he stroked the tawny hide of a fallen doe—which sharply contrasted with the time he touched a feral hog and was startled by how bristly it was— these are the small snippets I cherish.

When it comes right down to it, it's the peace and serenity of the fields and woods I love. I've hunted all over the country—in most states, in fact—and it never gets old. Bringing Beau up as a hunter is my idea of a seriously good time.

Aside from the meat, why do you hunt? I do it for the sheer zen of the outdoors. The zen and the smiles.

MORE BOOKS

Here are other books you can read by these authors. We hope that if you have enjoyed this book, you would tell at least three people about it. We know that folks who don't like a thing tell everyone about it, so if we can ask you to tell three when you liked it, it would help out the authors more than you'd think for such a small thing.

JL CURTIS ALSO WRITES, AMONG OTHER THINGS, THE BELL Chronicles, book one being *Showdown on the River*

La Vaughn Vanderburg Kemnow also wrote *Alaska Bush Mother*

Denton Salle writes the Avatar Wizard series, beginning with *Sworn to the Light*

Kelly Grayson wrote *En Route: A Paramedic's Stories of Life, Death, and Everything in Between*

LA Behm II wrote *Martian Aria* among others

Doug Irvin edited *Space Force: Building the Legacy*

Karen Myers writes The Hounds of Annwn, which begins with *To Carry the Horn*

Warren Vanderburg's memoirs and tales can be found in *Confessions of a Poacher*

Rodney Smith also writes the Galactic Republic series, beginning with *Like Seed Cast on Fertile Ground*

Lawdog also appears in *The Ratel Saga, Taskforce Chiweenie,* and *Astrolizards*

Kat Stevens writing as Kat Ainsworth authored *Handgun Hunting*

And of course, this is the second volume of hunting stories, the first one if you missed it is *How Not to Shoot Fish, and other Deer That Got Away*

NOTES

9. FORTYMILE CARIBOU BLUES BY BRENNAN HANKINS

1. Don't Drink And Drive, ya numpties! Ya might hit a bum and spill your beer!

www.ingramcontent.com/pod-product-compliance
Lightning Source LLC
Chambersburg PA
CBHW071325140726
47996CB00005B/1820